GOLF—BEGIN THE RIGHT WAY

The Story of Golf
Golf with the Experts
More Golf with the Experts
Golf Secrets of the Masters
(with Geoffrey Cousins)

GOLF—
BEGIN THE RIGHT WAY

TOM SCOTT

with line illustrations by Alex Hay

DAVID & CHARLES
NEWTON ABBOT   LONDON
NORTH POMFRET   VANCOUVER

0 7153 65703

© Tom Scott, 1974

Set in 11 on 13pt Times New Roman and printed in
Great Britain at the St Ann's Press Park Road Altrincham
Cheshire WA14 5QQ
for David & Charles (Holdings) Limited
South Devon House Newton Abbot Devon

Published in the United States of America by
David & Charles Inc
North Pomfret Vermont 05053 USA

Published in Canada by
Douglas David & Charles Limited
3645 McKechnie Drive West Vancouver B.C.

CONTENTS

FOREWORD

Throughout this book, which has been written specially for beginners, I have stressed that the best way to take up the game —no matter what age—is to go and have lessons from a professional. But for lack of time or money, or because of possible embarrassment, many people do not have lessons when they take up golf, so perhaps what I have written in these pages will be of special benefit to them. I hope that it will also be of interest, and perhaps of some help, to all who are thinking of playing golf as well as those who have already started or who, perhaps, do not play very often.

To play golf really well it is necessary to go out on the course at frequent intervals, and that is particularly so for those who have not yet become skilled. They will not yet have reached the stage of playing each stroke in such a way that it becomes completely automatic. Indeed many people play golf for a lifetime and never reach that stage.

For the unskilled or semi-skilled, long absence from golf is bad because they will have forgotten what they did the last time they played. Sometimes, after being away from the game, you play remarkably well for a time but then, when a bad shot comes along, you start thinking about all manner of things and your game then goes. So, if you want to reach a reasonable standard at golf, try to play as often as you can.

Golf is an individual game and, that being so, what I have written will not make everybody who reads it a good golfer. But in the simplest terms I have tried to give every reader a sound foundation on which to build. And once a golfer's game has a sound foundation, then he or she is well on the way to reaching a good standard, even a very good standard.

Once you start playing golf, or having started it are becoming fairly proficient at it, you will find that it provides a great challenge, a challenge made all the more formidable because you are on your own. And that is one of the reasons why golf is such an enjoyable game.

Had it not been so it would not have survived through the centuries until now, when it is said to be the fastest growing participant game in the world. Except in one or two Communist countries, golf is played throughout the globe and I believe it is only a matter of time until it will be played in every country.

The Russians, for instance, have departed from team games to the extent that their tennis players are now world ranked. When they take up golf, we can expect them to do so with enthusiasm and with a burning desire to turn out some of the very best.

That, of course, will not affect you much as an ordinary player, but at least it will be a reminder to you that the game you play is one that is ever attracting more and more devotees.

Golf has given millions of people enormous pleasure and you, too, will find it enjoyable, even although there will be times when you feel it is the most frustrating and hateful game in the world. But that will only be after you have been playing very badly. The feeling will soon pass and then you will be again out on the course with new theories and even greater enthusiasm than before.

Chalfont St Giles   TOM SCOTT
1974

1. YOU CAN START GOLF AT ANY AGE

As editor of the weekly magazine, *Golf Illustrated*, I often receive snapshots from doting parents showing one of their offspring holding a golf club at some tender age of perhaps two or three years. True that in all but a few instances the child will be holding the club with the left hand below the right, which is the 'wrong' way to hold the club even though to the youngster shown in the photograph it must obviously have been the natural way.

But never mind, the main thing is that the parents are delighted that their offspring are already showing an aptitude for a game which they themselves have probably enjoyed for a number of years, and perhaps, too, they see in the young hopefuls budding stars who will one day achieve a higher standard at golf than they were ever able to attain.

That is one end of the scale. At the other end there are many golfers of both sexes who play golf into their eighties. Some remarkable players even play after they have reached their nineties. Only recently I lunched at the Son Vida Club in Majorca with a man who was seventy-six years old. He had just finished a round on the tough, sometimes hilly course and was as 'fresh as when he started. The remarkable thing about him, apart from his physical condition, was that he did not start playing the game until after he was fifty.

He was a Welshman and, like many another of his countrymen, had been a rugby player in his youth. He gave that up at the age of thirty, and then took up tennis. Eventually the time came for him to lay down his racket and then he looked around for some other game he could play.

Golf was an obvious choice, and he told me that he enjoyed every moment of it and had succeeded in getting his handicap down to a respectable fourteen. There have been many other and more spectacular cases of golfers who started the game late in life and got their handicap to a very low figure, much lower than my friend at Son Vida, but his performance will well serve my purpose, which is to stress that golf can be started late in life and played with enjoyment for many years.

Then there are those who start quite young and continue for as long as it is physically possible for them to play. They, I fancy, form the majority of those who play golf, and their numbers have greatly increased in recent years as a result of the strenuous efforts which have been made to encourage more youngsters to take up the game.

For many years schools were not enthusiastic about their pupils playing golf. Team games such as rugby, soccer and cricket were the only games allowed, the theory being that team games taught the participants not to be selfish and develop the team spirit. Perhaps because at least some team games have become tarnished in recent years by the unsportsmanlike behaviour of the players, there has been a decided change of heart on the part of headmasters, many of whom have now come round to the way of thinking that golf has much to offer as a character builder. In golf, as in life, you are on your own. When a decision has to be made about which shot has to be played only the person playing the shot can decide. And as far as you are concerned, you are that person.

Then, again, nobody who has ever played golf would deny that it calls for a strong sense of character. To play golf well it is an advantage to be strong physically, but it is even more important to have the right mental outlook. From the time the game began, well over three hundred years ago, much has been said and written about the mental side of golf, and in all these years no one, so far as I know, has ever claimed that the physical side is more important than the mental side. Not, of course, that the physical side can be discounted. To be able to play one round of golf, and certainly two rounds of golf in a day, one has to be moderately fit, although it has to be said that many physically handicapped people do play two rounds a day. The outstanding example is Group-Captain Douglas Bader, the legless former Royal Air Force pilot, who is an enthusiastic and able golfer. There are many others, not quite so severely handicapped perhaps, who play golf, and play it well. For such people to do so requires not only physical stamina but also mental courage of a high order.

So we come back to the character-building properties of golf, and the reason—or at least one reason—why more and more schools allow pupils to play golf in school hours. So far as Britain is concerned, few schools have yet placed golf on the official sports curriculum, but a start has been made and there are indications that more schools will follow before long.

Another reason why golf is becoming more popular in schools is that various bodies have done much work to foster enthusiasm for the game among young people. Considerable work in this direction has been achieved in Britain by the Golf Foundation, a non-profit-making organisation formed some years ago for just such a purpose and corresponding to a somewhat similar body already in being in the United States. After a number of articles on its aims had been published in *Golf Illustrated*, the idea was taken up by that great professional, Henry Cotton, and several leading members of the golf trade. Now as a result, thousands of boys and girls are able to have tuition from golf coaches at school. A few municipalities also provide coaching facilities for novice golfers.

So now, what with school coaching and the numerous youngsters who take naturally to the game, especially in Scotland where there are so many public courses, there is quite a considerable flow of young people into golf. Their problem in the future will be to find courses on which to play. More and more courses are coming into being but the demand is already much greater than the available supply, a state of affairs which is likely to continue for a long time to come. But despite the fact that most clubs have more members than they know how to cope with, they are usually sympathetic to young players and prepared to offer them cheap terms. Older men and women wishing to take up the game are not so fortunate, and may have to search round for a club which they can join. If they fail in this, the only alternative is to play on a public course until such time as they are able to join a private club.

Those whose schooldays are behind them, in some cases long behind them, do not take up golf for the purpose of character building. They take it up, perhaps because they have had to give up a sport more suitable for younger men, or maybe because they have no aptitude for more active sports. Whatever the reason, they are likely to find the game both enjoyable and challenging. People can play golf for years without ever becoming very proficient at it, and yet still find it enjoyable because it gives them exercise and fresh air and also enables them to meet and enjoy the company of many people in various walks of life. Golf is a great leveller and all who play it, no matter their social or financial status, have to endure its frustrations as well as enjoying its pleasures.

Most golfers are confirmed optimists and though there are times when they threaten to quit the game for ever, the phase quickly passes and they are soon back again, convinced that the future holds better things for them. And, of course, it does. Another great thing from which beginners at golf can gain comfort is that no matter how badly they play, they will always see others around them who are playing even worse, or so it seems. It is remarkable how satisfying that can be. It also means that no one should ever feel embarrassed at starting the game. Everybody has to start sometime, and there are not many who take to the game in such a manner as to play well at the outset.

Golfers, in general, fall into two well defined categories. One category includes those who are determined to play golf really well, and who, to achieve that end, are prepared to devote much time to playing and practising. The second category are those who merely take up golf for the healthy exercise and enjoyment it gives. But no matter which category you belong to, the best way to start is to see a professional and to have a sufficient number of lessons from him to ensure that when you do start going out on the course you know the rudiments of the game and can hit the ball with a modest degree of accuracy. There are, however, some things which no professional can impart to a pupil—how to play certain shots, for instance—and these can only be learned by experience. But it will help if you know how to go about playing them, and this book will tell you just that. It will also help to make you familiar with the various clubs, and the use or uses to which each one can be put.

It may be there are those who wish to take up golf but have no idea how to set about it. Such people are probably in the minority, as most decide to play golf because they either live near a golfcourse or have friends who play. For them, starting golf is comparatively easy. For the others who have problems, a visit to their nearest golfcourse is recommended. There they can ask to see the professional or the secretary who will gladly give them advice, while the professional will also be pleased to suggest the right clubs to purchase.

One important side to golf not previously mentioned is the social side. Golf clubs vary in their social activities, but almost all have social gatherings of some sort or another—bridge, dinners, dances and suchlike—and these activities are particularly useful in helping members to get to know each other. Many people new to a district have had their lives made more pleasant by joining the local golf club. This may not be the best reason for taking up golf, but it is an important one all the same and not to be discounted.

Golf, then, has much to offer in many different ways. You can start playing it when you are quite young. You can start it when you are quite old. When you do start playing it, it gives lasting enjoyment and enables you to make many friendships which will last as long as you live. Few games can claim to do that to the same degree.

2. SOMETHING ABOUT THE CLUBS

Before describing the various clubs and when they should be used, it should be stressed that golf, like all other games and sports, has its rules and the first thing anyone starting golf should do is to make herself or himself familiar with these rules. There are sets of rules displayed in all golf clubs and, in the United Kingdom, the offices of the Royal Insurance Group supply, on request, a small booklet which beginners will find most helpful.

Now to the golf clubs, the implements with which the game is played. The maximum number of clubs which can be carried during a round is fourteen. There is no particular reason why the number should have been fixed at fourteen, but it was arrived at to stop players carrying vast numbers of clubs which they did in the 1920s. Sets comprising the fourteen clubs can be purchased from any golf professional, who will also advise a customer as to the weight and type of club which will suit him best. Golf clubs, however, are expensive, good ones costing anything from £5 to £10 or even more, so that many beginners content themselves with buying what are termed 'short sets', which usually comprise seven clubs. That number is perfectly adequate. In some cases a golf professional may be able to supply second-hand clubs, and if they are in good condition these may well be worth considering.

Let us start with a full set. In the old days clubs had names, but that practice has died out and now, except perhaps for the driver, the wedge and the putter, clubs have numbers. Usually a set comprises four woods, nine irons and a putter, the woods being numbered from No 1 (the driver) to No 4 for the most lofted of the woods. The irons are usually numbered from No 2 to No 9, with a wedge and putter to make up the fourteen. Some sets contain a No 1 iron but generally only the best professionals use such a club as more humble players find it difficult to play. A short set of seven clubs usually comprises two woods, perhaps a No 2 and a No 3 and four irons, (Nos 3, 5, 7 and 9) plus a putter.

As suggested by their name, the 'woods' usually have heads made of wood although in recent years, due to a shortage of the right material, some have had heads made of a synthetic substance. The 'irons' have heads made of iron, except for some putters which can have heads of brass or aluminium or iron. Almost all shafts nowadays are made of steel, although aluminium and glass fibre is occasionally used, but not so much in Britain as in the United States.

Now let us go through the range of clubs starting with the driver, or No 1 wood. This has a longer shaft than any of the other woods, and less loft in the face. The reason for this is that when you 'drive off' from the teeing ground at each hole and the wood is being used, the ball is placed on a wooden or plastic teepeg which is pushed into the ground. That being so there is no necessity to have loft on the face of the club. The No 2 wood is a fraction shorter in the shaft and has a small amount of loft on the face. Its purpose is to play long shots from a good lie on the fairway. It is not an easy club to play but can be most effective, for remember many golf holes are more than 500 yards in length.

The No 3 wood has a shaft slightly shorter than the No 2 and the face has even more loft. This club, which used to be known as a 'spoon', is most versatile and a great favourite with average golfers. The distance with which the ball can be hit with it is a shade less than with the No 2 but it can be played from indifferent fairway lies with a high degree of accuracy. It can also be played from good lies in the rough. The other wood, the No 4, has a good deal of loft and can be played from lies from which it might well be dangerous to play its big brothers.

Because individual golfers hit the ball varying distances, and because each player's shots can vary anyway, it is not easy to say what distances each of the wood clubs can cover. But with

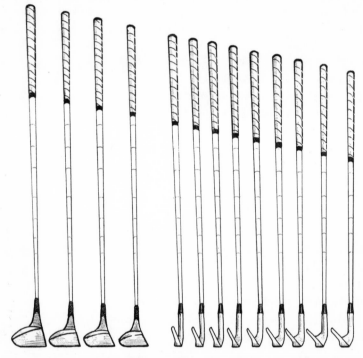

The woods and the irons: (left to right) Nos 1–4 woods and Nos 1–9 irons; note that the loft on the faces of the irons increases and length of shaft decreases in ascending order of numbers

a little experience every golfer is able to decide what lies within his capacity, and to exercise judgement accordingly. It should be remembered that few beginners at the game hit the ball further than they intend and that when a really long shot is called for it is not often that the ball goes as far as was hoped. Certainly, however, every beginner will find that the No 3 wood and the No 4 wood are safe clubs to play, and effective as well.

We can discount the No 1 iron, rarely used by any but the best golfers, and start with the No 2 iron. Iron clubs, as with the woods, are graded by their degree of loft. For example, the No 2 iron has only a small amount of loft, the No 3 iron more loft, the No 4 iron even more loft and so on. And as the numbers increase the shafts become a little shorter. There is no more satisfactory shot in the whole of the game than a well hit No 2 or No 3 iron into the wind, but because the heads of the Nos 3 and 4 woods have a more solid look about them many beginners will prefer to use them instead of the irons. In theory, of course, the ball should go further when hit with the woods than with the irons. It is really all a matter of confidence.

The No 2 iron is for use from good lies on the fairway, the No 3 from lies which are not quite as good; not good enough, for instance, for using a No 4 wood. Some people may differ about this, and again all one can say is that beginners will learn from experience which club they can use to the best effect.

Coming now to the No 4 iron, which has a fair loft, the distance one is from the green comes into the scheme of things. It can also be played from not very good lies in the rough. Like its neighbour the No 4 wood, it is a great favourite with those who have not had much experience at the game because it gets the ball into the air and sends it a reasonable distance.

And if that is true of the No 4, it is doubly true of the No 5 iron which, in bygone days, used to be called a 'mashie'. Some of the great stars of the past were adept at playing this club and their accuracy with it was astounding. It can be used for getting out of trouble and it can be used for playing shots to the green from quite a distance away. Many careful golfers also use it for playing quite short shots to the green when there is no great obstacle between where the ball is lying and the green itself. This shot, once very popular, was known as a 'run-up shot'. It has gone out of fashion nowadays but on occasion it can be played with excellent results.

In the main, the Nos 6 and 7 irons are for use when the green is within their distance—the distance depending on the skill of the player—although, as with all lofted clubs, they can also be of immense help in getting out of rough or from bad lies in general. The clubs, it will be noted, are now beginning to have quite a degree of loft on their faces, which means that it is possible to get the ball high into the air with them. Like the No 5 iron, average golfers find the No 7 iron a most useful club and it is not a bad thing when starting the game to try to become really proficient with it and perhaps also with the No 3 wood and the No 5 iron, for these clubs are the backbone of many a player's game. By doing so you will become confident in their use and, having once mastered them, you can then do the same with the other clubs in your bag. This unorthodox plan is especially useful if at the outset you have invested in a full set of fourteen clubs. Quite obviously, if you start using them all it is going to be some considerable time before you become reasonably expert with any one of them. It is this getting to know your clubs quicker which makes sense of starting golf with a 'short set', which can be added to as and when you wish.

A disadvantage of the short set is that it will be without a wedge or a sand iron, and so you will have to make do with a No 8 or No 9 iron for getting out of deep trouble in the rough, from recovering from bunkers, or as the Americans call them, 'sand traps'. A full set includes a No 8 iron and a No 9. Both are what might be called recovery clubs, the No 9 having a deeper face than the No 8. They are also used for playing little shots to the green, particularly where there is some hazard such as a hill or a bunker between the spot where the ball is lying and the flag. Faced with that situation, the ball has not only to be got into the air quickly but also made to stop fairly quickly when it lands on the green. Clubs such as the No 8 and the No 9 have heavy heads as well as lofted faces which means that the weight of the head going through and under the ball helps to get the ball into the air. It will not be long before you discover that playing these lofted shots to the green is an art, and that if played correctly they can save many strokes in a round of golf. Remember that a bad little shot to the green, like a missed short putt, counts just as much as the longest shot you have ever hit. More than that, bad little shots can be most demoralising.

The wedge has already been mentioned and it is of the same family as the No 9 iron. It is equally deeply lofted but has a flange on the sole, the purpose of which is to impart spin to the ball and also help to get the ball up when playing from very bad lies in the rough. It is the most powerful weapon in the golfing armoury, and because it is in a golfing sense, a lethal club, it is most difficult to play. In addition to relying upon it to get them out of trouble, good golfers use the wedge for approach shots to the green, knowing that the spin it imparts to the ball will result in the ball stopping almost dead in its tracks when it lands on the green.

It is not advisable for beginners to start using a wedge—if they possess one—until they become thoroughly familiar not only with it but with every other club in their bag. It is not an easy club to use and there will be time enough to play wedge shots after all the other and less difficult clubs have been mastered. As we have seen, clubs like a No 3 or No 4 wood and a No 5 and a No 7 iron have a reasonable amount of loft—not too much—and with them you can get the ball into the air, and if you have hit it well you will be surprised just how far it goes. This may be something of a 'safety first' policy, but you will find from experience that it makes good sense all the same.

Now we come to what many golfers maintain is the most important club of all—the putter. It is quite different from all the others, and is mainly for use when you have reached the green. It can, however, also be used from a lie just off the green when there is no obstacle between the spot where the ball is lying and the green. The American term for this unorthodox but effective shot is the 'Texas wedge', presumably because Texans are said to be very shrewd people and just a little bit more artful than their fellow citizens from other states.

Putters are included in most sets of clubs, though many

experienced golfers prefer to use one which has become a firm favourite over the years. Other golfers disappointed at their lack of success with one putter will often change over to some other type, of which there are many. The new putter may prove successful for only a short period and then they will make yet another change, forgetting, of course, that it is not the club

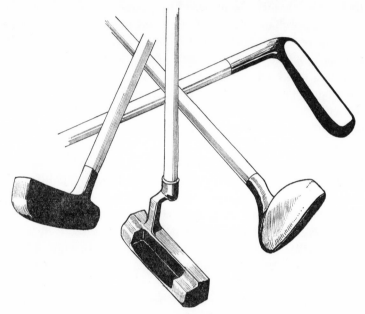

Four different types of putters

which is to blame for their frustration but the player who is using it.

It is quite impossible to say which type of putter is best for a particular person, but it can be said that for the majority of people it should neither be too light nor too heavy. The two main kinds of putters are those which have the shaft joined to the head at one end or almost at one end (a blade putter), and those which have the shaft joined to the head in the centre. The latter are known as centre-shafted putters and are perhaps more favoured nowadays than any other type.

Generally, the best thing that beginners can do is to find a putter with which they feel comfortable and then stick to it, at least long enough to give it an extended trial. In the main, it can be said that all the great putters have been those who have stuck to the same putter for years. Continual experiments may be successful for a time but, more likely than not, after a spell, they cease to work the expected wonders.

As the purchase of a set of golf clubs involves an appreciable cash outlay it is essential that, as far as humanly possible, the correct choice is made at the very outset, except, perhaps, when a second-hand set can be picked up at a very attractive price. Such bargains may not always be entirely suitable. For instance, light clubs are better for beginners than heavy ones, and the clubs offered second-hand may be heavy clubs. To be sure of getting a set that will really suit you, you would be well advised to go to a professional and buy your clubs from him. But having said that let me add that some old clubs bought cheaply, or which have been received as a gift, will be quite good enough to start with, and will serve their purpose until the player concerned has become enthusiastic and reasonably proficient at the game.

It all really depends on how keen the beginner is to improve and, of course, how he or she is placed financially at the particular moment. Remember there is other equipment to buy such as shoes (with spikes), waterproofs and umbrella, perhaps sweaters and a left-hand glove. This latter piece of golf equipment is not essential but is worn by most golfers to give them a firmer grip with their left hand, which many teachers claim is essential in order to play golf well. It should, however, be pointed out that many fine champions have never used a left-hand glove and do not advocate it. A beginner will soon find out if it is for him, and in any case it is not an expensive item. The cost of golf equipment varies quite a bit and you may have to shop around to get the items which suit your purse.

There is one small but constantly growing category of golfers who have not been mentioned in this discussion about clubs.

These are the left-handed players. Many years ago, writing with the left hand at school was frowned upon, with the result that there were not many left-handed people about and certainly not many left-handed golfers. But now scholars and students can write with their left hands if they choose and so there are more natural 'lefties' about. Certainly there are many more left-handed golfers in the game than there were some years ago.

The selection of clubs available to them is not as great as that offered to right-handed players but most of the leading golf-club manufacturers do make left-handed clubs. Many golf professionals also stock them or, if they do not, they can readily obtain them. One left-handed golfer of the highest class is the former British Open Champion, Bob Charles from New Zealand, and there are many other left-handers who have achieved great success at the game. So if you are a natural left-hander in everything you do, if you feel more comfortable playing golf that way, go ahead and do so.

Unfortunately, as there are far more right-handed golfers than left-handed ones this book, in common with all but a few golf books ever published, has had to be written with the majority in mind. Some left-handed players will say that for left-handers everything should be reversed, while others maintain that this is not so and that they have their own special problems. The best that I have been able to do is to write the book in simple terms in the hope that left-handers will benefit from it to some extent. After all, the basic problems with which golfers have to contend—and the emphasis is very much on the 'basic'—are the same for all whether right-handers or left-handers.

3. STANDING UP TO IT

There are experts who say that the grip—that is the way you hold the club—is the most important thing in golf. Others say that the stance—the way you stand to hit the ball—is the most important. I think that they are both most important. Having said that, let us start with the stance since this is the first positive step you take in playing golf. Naturally, you will be holding the club when you step up to hit the ball, but the first thing you do is to take up your stance preparatory to playing your very first shot.

The object of standing up to the ball, or taking up your stance as it is commonly called, is to enable you to hit the ball as far and as straight as you can, except, of course, for shorter shots, when the object is to hit the ball as accurately as you can to cover the required distance. To do either of those two things you must be so balanced on your feet that when, in making the stroke, the time comes for the balance to be shifted from one foot to another you can do it in such a manner as will enable you to make a good shot, as we shall see later.

Obviously, if throughout your stroke you have all the weight on one foot or the other, the attempt to hit the ball will be nothing less than disastrous. You have only to stand near the first tee of any golf club any Sunday morning and see for yourself. I will guarantee that a fair proportion of those driving off will have bad balance and because of that will not be good golfers. If there is one maxim about playing golf which is more true than any other, it is that when you stand up to hit the ball you must have good balance. Never forget that, because if you do the game will become much harder for you.

The first question in the matter of balance is how to stand. Many beginners at golf stand far too rigid. They feel that if they are rigid they will get more power into their shots. That is

(*Left*) Stance too rigid; (*right*) correct stance, flexed and forward

quite wrong. The knees should be slightly flexed (or bent, if you prefer it). Some golf teachers go so far as to say you should stand feeling that you could spring off the ground. I think that is a little too dramatic and prefer to say there should be a flexible or resilient feeling at the knees which gives a 'sitting down' position. But while as a result of that posture the upper part of the body will bend a little forward, there should be no crouching in the real sense of the word. There is bending forward but there should be no hunching up. In fact, the degree of bending forward will depend more on the distance you are standing from the ball rather than the slight easing at the knees.

To maintain perfect balance the feet must be apart. How far apart? That is not an easy question to answer. Many golf professionals say that, for the driver, the distance between the feet should be about the same as the width of the shoulders. I do not agree with that because what they are saying is that a short, stout golfer with enormous shoulders should have a very wide stance, and a golfer of six feet three inches with narrow shoulders should have a very narrow stance. No, there are too many golfers of different shapes and sizes for such a formula to work with everybody.

I prefer to think that the width between the feet at the address, as the stance is often called, should be comfortable. You can think vaguely in terms of the width of the shoulders as some kind of rough guide, but you will soon know if your stance is too wide because you will not be comfortable; you will feel strained. On the other hand, if the stance is too narrow you will feel cramped. That being so, obviously the right stance is somewhere between the two. This may all sound very like a compromise, which it is, and it will not be long before you find out that in golf there has to be much compromise as well as a considerable amount of improvisation. The great thing about the stance is that both feet should be firmly anchored to the ground. They will not be if they are too wide apart or too close to each other. Admittedly, there are many golfers with stances so unorthodox as to be laughable who can sometimes hit the ball quite well, but unless you are a very remarkable person you will never be a reasonably good golfer if you are completely unorthodox. And, anyway, who wants to be a freak?

We have seen, then, that the feet should be anchored to the ground, that the knees should be slightly flexed and that the feet should be comfortably apart. Remember, though, that so far we have been discussing the width of the stance from the point of view of the driver. As golf shafts become a little shorter as the numbers of the clubs increase, then so does the stance narrow ever so slightly, until when you are playing, say, a No 8 iron, the stance will be quite narrow.

The next thing to decide is how far one should stand from the ball. There is the old joke of the golfer who said his fault in golf was standing too near to the ball after he had hit it—a joke, it is to be hoped, which will never apply to you.

There is no set distance you have to be away from the ball because of the great variation in the size and build of golfers, and the importance of feeling comfortable. The best way to determine your own correct distance is to lay the head of the club down behind the ball—to do this you hold the club by the grip, of course. Then move back far enough for the arms to be stretched out but not to the point that they are rigid. The hands should be about four inches from the body. I have already said that the knees should be flexed but that you should not be hunched forward. If you do the former and are bent forward but not hunched, then you are about right. With the shorter-shafted clubs you will, of course, be nearer the ball. You must be, because if you stayed the same distance away as for the driver you would be bent almost double—which would neither be good for your golf nor your stomach muscles, to say nothing of your back.

The next question is where the ball should be in relation to the feet. The general theory is that, for the driver, the ball should be in a straight line outwards from the left heel, and that as the clubs progressively become more lofted the ball should be further back towards the right foot until, when playing a No 8 iron, it should be just about opposite the right heel. It is not for me to question seriously the majority of the experts, but in disagreeing to some extent with this practice I have on my side such a thinker of the game as Max Faulkner. Although now in the senior golfer bracket, Max still has as good a swing as ever he had, which proves that his methods stand up to the years, which after all is something that would satisfy most people taking up the game. He maintains that this idea of having the ball opposite the left heel for long shots and opposite the right heel for short shots is overdone. He thinks that, for most of the clubs, the position of the ball in relation to the feet should vary only marginally and that only for the very short shots should it be changed from its basic position, which he says should be about equi-distant from each foot. I think this method will find favour with many people for whom having the ball opposite or nearly opposite the left heel for the longer shots is something of a strain.

The object in golf being to hit the ball in a certain direction, you must obviously stand facing that direction, which in golf language is called 'the intended line of flight'. This means that while you are trying to play to the green it is not always possible to take the most direct route because of obstacles in the way, or perhaps because the ground slopes down from one side or the other. In the latter case, it would be prudent to play to the high side.

How then should the feet be placed? Many agree that the feet should be 'square', in other words that if you laid a golf club down on the ground, the end nearest the hole would be pointing exactly where you intended the ball to go, whether it be straight to the pin, or, because of hazards, to the right or left of the fairway. Some experts go for a slightly open stance, that is one in which the left foot is drawn slightly back from the intended line of flight. There is nothing much against this method, which many people use, but the trouble is that the ground from which you have to play shots, even on some tees, is not always level, so that the left foot is apt to stray a little further back than you intended. Therefore, on balance, I would recommend a square stance, at least until such time as you know more about the game.

When you are watching other golfers play you will notice that many of them, particularly those who are short in stature, stand with their left foot pushed further forward to the intended line of flight than the right foot. This is known as a closed stance and is not to be recommended because it can lead to hooking

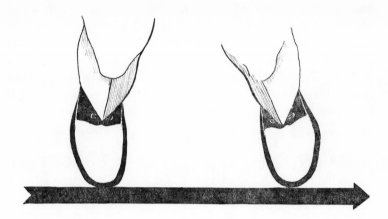

Square stance

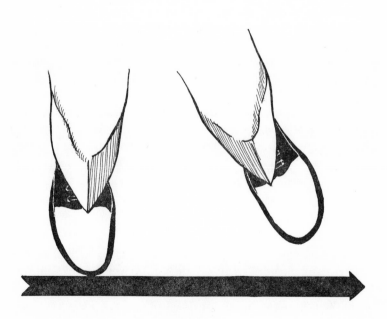

Open stance

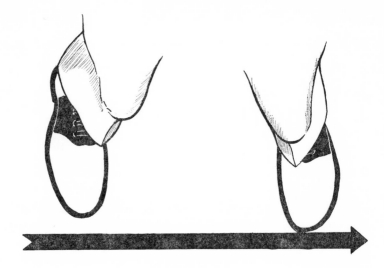

Closed stance

the ball, which means bending it round to the left where it is likely to find trouble.

To go back over the things to remember about the stance: first you should tell yourself over and over again that you must feel comfortable. Never mind all those people you see out on a golf course looking more like contortionists than players of what should be a simple game. It may well be that they are able to play some good shots, but if you watched them all the time you would find they played an awful lot of bad ones as well.

So be relaxed, have your knees flexed and do not stand too near the ball or you will restrict your movements. On the other hand, do not stand too far away from it or you may stretch forward to such an extent as to lose your balance. And balance is what the stance is all about. Finally, the feet should be placed so that a straight line drawn across the toes is the direction in which you hope the ball will go.

4.   GETTING TO GRIPS

Just as the stance is important because the feet are the only parts of the body in contact with the ground, so it is true to say that the hands are equally important because they are the only parts of the body in contact with the club. Henry Cotton, who won the British Open Championship three times, has always maintained that in the whole spectrum of golf the hands are by far of the greatest importance.

Holding the club is usually called 'the grip', though this, I feel, is apt to give the impression that one should hold the club as a vice would hold a bolt. This is not correct. The hold on the club should only be firm enough to give you complete control of its movement as you take it back and up and bring it down again.

But let us first examine the three different ways of holding the club: the overlapping grip (which is by far the most popular), the interlocking grip and the two-handed grip. The overlapping, or Vardon grip, is so called because it was first popularised by Harry Vardon who won the British Open Championship six times, more often than any other man. In this grip, the right hand is well over on top of the clubshaft so that the little finger curls round the first finger of the left hand, which is also well over the top of the clubshaft.

This 'over the top of the shaft' business cannot be stressed too much because this is where so many beginners go wrong. They simply will not press the hands together, for the most part having the right hand much too far under the shaft. This is because they are holding the shaft with the palms rather than

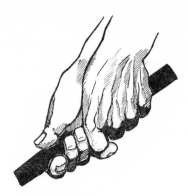

The overlapping grip

with the fingers. Holding the shaft with the fingers is essential no matter which type of grip you are using.

The second grip is the interlocking, now not nearly as popular as it once was. In fact, it may be said to be almost completely out of fashion. Those who do or did use it claimed that its merit

The interlocking grip

lay in keeping the hands more in unison with each other. As is suggested by the word 'interlocking', this grip has the little finger of the right hand interlocked with the first finger of the left hand. I think it unfortunate that this grip has lost public favour because it seems to me to have the great advantage of keeping the hands more on top of the shaft and so making the greater use of the fingers quite natural. In this I may be old-fashioned but old fashioned ways of doing things are not neccessarily wrong ways. The third grip is the two-handed grip, in which the hands are separate from each other, neither inter-locking nor overlapping.

The two-handed grip

So much for the different kinds of grip. The next step is to see how to go about putting one or other of them into practice. For the purpose of this exercise we will take the overlapping grip as the example because it is the one most generally used.

Standing up in the manner described in the last chapter, you take hold of the club and lay the grip diagonally across the palm and fingers of the left hand in a position near the top of the first finger to the base of the inside of the palm. You then close the fingers of the hand round the club, pressing the rest of the hand over on top of the shaft (ie, that part of the shaft nearest your face). If this is done correctly and you are holding the club in the proper position down the shaft, about an inch of the shaft should be shown past the left-hand side of the wrist. If the left hand is far enough over, the thumb should be a little to the right of the shaft as you look down. You should also be able to see two knuckles of the first two fingers of the left hand and

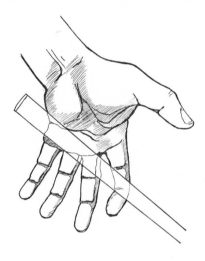

Left hand taking up the overlapping grip

to notice that there is a V formed by the base of the thumb and the first finger. If this all sounds complicated, study the diagrams on the grip.

Now to the right hand, which has to be folded round the club, or rather the fingers of the right hand have to be folded round. The little finger of the right hand is placed on top of the first finger of the left hand, or perhaps it would be better to say that it should be curled round the first finger of the left hand. The next move is to close the other three fingers of the right hand round the club with the base of the thumb well on top of the club and pressing against the base of the first finger of the left hand. The thumb of that hand should be down the shaft of the club.

Many beginners find that this 'hand on top' business feels uncomfortable to start with and relapse into the fatal fault of the right hand under the shaft. And that, my friends, is the quickest way to hook a ball that I know of. So, no matter how uncomfortable this grip feels at first, persevere with it and rest assured that it really will come right in the end.

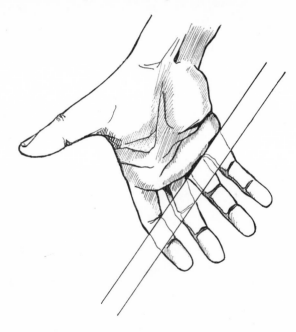

Right hand taking up the overlapping grip

There remains only the question of how tightly to grip the club. A most important part of golf is the downswing, when the club has been taken back and is being brought down prior to hitting the ball. The left hand is then in command, so it can be said that although the right hand is important in the golf swing, the left hand is at least dominant during a vital stage in it. That being so, the grip of the left hand must be firm, but not tight. Try to think of guiding with your left hand one of those shopping baskets on wheels through a crowd in a shopping precinct. What you do then is to grip the handle just tightly enough to control the contraption. So it is with the golf grip. Firm enough to control, but not tight enough to be a strain.

5. SETTING UP THE STROKE

Playing a golf shot is not just a case of holding the club, adopting a stance and then hitting the ball without further delay. There is a good deal more to it than that. You have to 'address' the ball—that is, to get yourself ready to play the shot. It might be called planning the shot, for the period between taking up the stance and actually commencing the stroke is the time when you concentrate, become relaxed and finally wind up to the act of hitting the ball.

The first thing to do is to check your grip and your stance. If a golfer's grip and stance were to remain constant during their golfing lifetime, golf would be relatively simple. But they don't. Through familiarity or carelessness, call it what you will, the hands do change their position on the club shaft without you being aware of it. So, just as a car needs a service check now and again, so does your golf grip. The same applies to the position of the feet. The positions of one or other, or both, are apt to change marginally, and when that happens it can lead to quite a number of faults. This changing of hand and foot positions occurs perhaps more with fairway shots than with shots from the tee, the reason being that the fairway shots are being played from varying kinds of lies and the position in which the ball is lying dictates not only the choice of clubs but also how the shot is to be played.

We have already agreed that when you stand up preparatory to hitting the ball, the great thing is to be comfortable. Any hint of rigidity or tension will act against you hitting a good shot, whether it be from the tee or from the fairway. You must be comfortable. Now to decide where you are going to hit the ball. On a tight hole, where there are hazards on the left, for instance, it would be foolish to hit the ball to that side of the fairway. The obvious line is one which is going to keep you clear of trouble and that is to the right. You therefore take up your stance accordingly, with the left foot more forward than the right.

As well as watching carefully the position of the feet, there is the position of the head to consider. Many experts say that the chin should be aimed at a spot just behind the ball, and it is good advice inasmuch as it helps the player to anchor the head. It also means that the right shoulder will be a little lower than the left, which is correct. I like the expression 'anchor' because for years and years people have been talking about keeping the head absolutely still during the golf swing. I do not believe that the head can be kept absolutely still when playing a golf shot, and if you watch closely a film of a golfer in action you will surely notice that there is a slight movement of the head. But I certainly do agree that an effort should be made to keep the head as still as possible, because if you do not consciously do so then the chances are that the head will be lifted. That means that the eye will be taken off the ball, and one certain thing about golf is that you are unlikely to hit the ball correctly if you are not looking at it.

Now to the position of the hands. We know that they should be holding the shaft of the club on top. And, again, this does not mean at the end of the shaft—the distance from the end can be about an inch—but on top of the shaft as you look down on it. But where should the hands be in relation to the ball? Should they be behind it, level with it or in front of it? I plump for them being in front of it. And the way you achieve this position is to see that your left arm and the clubshaft are in a straight line as you put the sole of the club on the ground just behind the ball, then press your hands to the left. Some experts maintain that the exception to this rule is when playing from a tee with the ball resting on a teepeg. But that, I feel, tends to make things unnecessarily complicated and I believe that what

is good for fairway shots is also good for teeshots. Having the
hands in front of the ball gives a certain amount of leverage,
and at the same time helps to strengthen the feeling that you
are in complete control of the club.

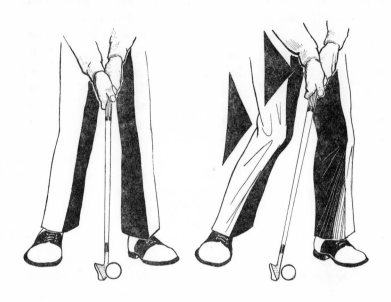

The 'forward press', with right knee flexed slightly inwards

Having settled the position of the feet, the head and the hands
and feeling thoroughly comfortable, the next and vital step is
to prepare to commence the swing. If you have watched other
golfers in action you will have noticed that before they start
the swing they put the sole of the club down on the ground
behind the ball and that, especially on the tee, they put the sole
of the club also down in front of the ball. Some players may
do this once, some may do it more often. This action is popu-
larly known as the 'waggle', and is really to get the golfer in the
'mood', or in the right frame of mind to take back the clubhead.

It will be noticed, too, that in doing this the golfer will press the clubhead close into the back of the ball by moving his hands a little to the left and pushing the clubhead down. 'Squeeze' the clubhead might be an even more apt description than 'press', and to assist the 'squeeze' the right knee should be flexed slightly inwards. This is known as the 'forward press' and is what might be termed the springboard of the swing.

As well as getting you 'in the mood', the forward press also helps to ensure that the left hand is in command, for although golf is a two-handed game it is the left hand which is predominant. Golf cannot be played successfully without the left hand being in control, and indeed without the left arm and left side being firm.

Important though this mental and physical preparation is in helping to prevent the player from hurrying the shot, it does not mean that there should be a great deal of shuffling about before the golfer goes up to hit the ball. This merely gets the player into a confused state of mind, whereas, ideally, he should know just exactly what is to be done and how he is going to do it. There is an old saying in golf that if you don't bring your golf to the course you won't find it there. Perhaps that is a little too sweeping, for there is not a golfer born who will not try a little bit of experimenting. Basically, however, the way to successful golf is to find a sound method and to repeat it for every shot.

Easier said than done, perhaps, but the thinking behind it is sound, and if it is to be carried out then obviously the right frame of mind has to be attained. That is why the 'setting up' is important.

6. THE IMPORTANCE OF THE HANDS

One of golf's greatest arguments has always been about what starts off the swing. Is it the hands, the hips or the shoulders? It is all rather like which came first, the chicken or the egg? I have no hesitation in saying that it is the hands which start the whole thing, for the simple reason that they are in charge of the club. The hips can turn, the shoulders can turn, but if the hands are not the commanding factor in that turn nothing very much will happen.

Some people regard the wrists and hands merely as hinges, but that is surely not correct because a hinge is a free agent and does not apply power, say, to the opening or shutting of a door. It is the weight of the door which determines whether it opens or closes quickly. Therefore thinking of the hands in golf as a hinge does not make sense because they have to be in control of the club from start to finish.

That great teacher Ernest Jones, who was born in Kent and later went to the United States to become perhaps the finest golf coach of all time, has often expounded the fallacy of the much quoted golf expression, 'Let the clubhead do the work.' 'The clubhead', said Jones, 'will not do any work on its own. It has to be made to do it.' And it is the hands, coupled with other factors, which make the clubhead do the work required of it.

It is the hands which determine to a great extent the arc of the swing, particularly at the very start of the backswing when the clubhead is being taken away from the ball. If the hands are pulled in or pushed out then the whole backswing will go wrong, for it is the hands which decide how the club is to be brought down, and at what speed.

But before going on to the speed of the clubhead and the question of timing—which is really the co-ordination of all parts of the body—let me say something about the 'feel' of the hands, which to my mind is most important in the playing of good golf.

This matter of 'feel' is not very often written about, because it is such an individual thing and so difficult to explain. If you are a beginner at the game you will not have given it much thought but, later on, you may begin to wonder why on some occasions you can play golf quite well while on others you play badly. There will be many reasons for this, and one of them might well be because of the 'feel' of the hands on the clubshaft, or the lack of it.

There will surely be some days when you go to the golf club for a round, take the driver out of the bag for the first teeshot and everything feels fine because the club responds. But there will be other days when you take a hold of that same club and it feels like nothing but a piece of iron. We are often told that golf is 90 per cent mental and 10 per cent physical, and for want of any better explanation it would seem that this lack of 'feel', or response, has nothing to do with the club itself but is due to the fact that the person holding it is not mentally attuned to the occasion.

There can be several reasons for this. Possibly, and most likely, the player has either hurried to the club or been late in reaching the tee where partners are waiting. Or it may be, perhaps, that the golfer is not 100 per cent fit. In either case, this lack of 'feel' is a bad omen for the game to come, and unless the player calms down his golf is liable to suffer.

Another cause of this occasional lack of 'feel' may be that the grip is not right. It may be too firm, or not firm enough. Golfers, especially those comparatively new at the game, are all too prone to hold the club too much in the palms of their hands. By so doing, they lose a great amount of feeling because the palms are not nearly as sensitive as the fingers. When you do have one of these 'off days' and feel that all is not comfortable with the hands it is often a good idea to stand away from the ball and have a few waggles with the club. Never mind if the others on the tee look at you in some surprise. It is much better to risk a few patronising smiles than to go up to the ball knowing that you are not in the right frame of mind to hit it correctly. Feeling comfortable is all important, and part of being comfortable is the feeling that your hands are in full control of the club.

Paramount, however, though the hands are in the hitting of a golf ball, they cannot do it by themselves, but need assistance from other actions such as the turn of the hips, which act as the dynamo of the swing from first to last and help to provide the power finally unleashed when the ball is hit. But the hands are the controllers, or governers of the swing, and control the path of the club both during the backswing and the downswing.

And they do more, for as they control the path of the clubhead they also take up from the hips—and also the shoulders—the task of generating the maximum amount of power so that when it strikes the ball the clubhead will be moving as fast as you can possibly make it move while still retaining control. After the hands have taken the clubhead up to the top of the swing in the correct path or arc, they have to bring the clubhead down again in the correct arc and at the same time build up speed. In fact, they push the clubhead up and they pull it down. No matter how much power has been generated by turning the hips and shoulders, the clubhead would not come down unless the hands pulled it down in a manner which is fully controlled and fast as well.

Having done that, the hands have still another duty to perform. After the ball has been struck they take the club past where the ball lay in what is called the follow-through. It might seem impossible to prevent the clubhead following through after the ball has been struck in view of the momentum it will have gathered during the downswing, but there are some golfers who succeed in doing this because they punch the ball rather than hit it with a smooth, controlled action. To do this they must be extremely strong, but their strength alone will not be enough to hit the ball with the accuracy or length required.

Speaking in general terms, the complete arc of the swing from start to finish should be very close to a circle, except that after the stroke has been completed the hands should be high, with the club pointing upwards rather than back round the shoulders. A good follow-through, and by that is meant a follow-through with the hands held high, is the perfect end to the stroke and the chances are that if you finish like that you will have played a good shot.

So it can be said that the hands are important factors in the golf swing from start to finish, and that it is their co-operation with the arms, hips and shoulders which produces that last-minute rush into the ball which ensures that when the ball is hit the speed of the clubhead is at its fastest. If energy is expended before the moment of impact, and the clubhead is starting to lose momentum when the ball is hit, then the timing is wrong. The same thing applies if sufficient clubhead speed has not been worked up when the ball is hit. The clubhead must have reached its maximum speed when the ball is hit. Nothing else will do.

7. THE SWING FROM START TO FINISH

The swing, as everybody knows, is a continuous action, but for the purpose of examining it let us divide it in two parts, the backswing and the downswing. Both the backswing and the downswing have the same purpose—to provide the power to hit the ball. If you watch other golfers playing it will be clear even to the most inexperienced eye that many of them vary in the way they swing the club. This is so even among star golfers who achieve good results from swings which most experts would agree are unorthodox. But it is a good thing for beginners to remember that a simple, orthodox swing is the safest and best to cultivate because, having less to go wrong with it, it is easier to put right if faults develop.

The importance of co-ordination of the hands with other parts of the body, as stressed in the previous chapter, is evident at the very start of the backswing, because although it is the hands which start taking back the clubhead you will not get the club very far back or up without help from the hips and the shoulders. In other words, the hands and arms are the mediums by which the power generated by the hips and shoulders is transmitted to the club.

But that is not all. It is not only a matter of taking the clubhead back and bringing it down, but also of bringing it down so that at the moment of impact with the ball it is moving fast and is also square to the ball. If the clubhead is facing outwards at the moment of impact it stands to reason that the ball

will fly off to the right, or if it is facing inwards the ball will fly
off to the left. In either case the result could well be disastrous.

The first thing in getting a correct backswing is the 'takeaway',
or the first movement when the clubhead is being taken back
away from the ball. But before that you have to make up your
mind where the clubhead is going. And where it should be going

. . . .'neither too upright' (*left*) 'nor too flat' (*right*)

is neither too upright nor too flat. In other words, at the top of
the backswing the clubhead should not be pushed high into the
air (this can happen if the left elbow is bent), nor should it be
right round the shoulders.

The rub is to decide what is the right line and to do this it is
necessary to go back to the address—where you are standing up
to the ball. Then, as already explained, you are in a position
neither crouching nor too tense, and with the arms and the club

forming a straight line. The object is then to take the clubhead back quite naturally, so that at the top of the backswing the clubface is facing neither up to the sky nor down to the ground.

But let us start at the very beginning of the actual swing. Remember, the first thing to attend to is the forward press which gives you confidence and sets you up for the first movement of the backswing—the takeaway—that co-ordinated movement in which the hands, hips and shoulders are all involved. The worst fault of beginners is to try to lift the clubhead up immediately. This is unsound. The clubhead should be taken back along the ground for as long as you can take it without feeling strained. At this stage the arms are quite straight, and anything you hear from other golfers about 'cocking the wrists', which means breaking or bending the wrists, should be forgotten. If the wrists are bent too quickly and unnaturally, then the face of the club will open (ie, it will have changed from its original position) and when you want to bring the club down you will have to roll the wrists back into a position from which you can strike the ball square on its back. So two movements are involved to achieve something which can be achieved in one. And the less complicated you can make golf, the better.

The simplest and best way is to take the clubhead back as near to the ground as possible, keeping the arms straight until the time comes to lift up the clubhead, when the wrists will break quite naturally. The distance you take the clubhead back along the ground may be as much as three feet. Then, at that point, the wrists are the weak part of the body and as you turn your hips and take up the clubhead the wrists will break of their own accord. They cannot do anything else, because you would be conscious that they are being strained.

The continuing co-ordination of hands, hips and shoulders will cause the clubhead to go up and in the correct arc, and it is very important that the arc should be a wide one. If it is not wide, the breaking of the wrists very early in the backswing causes the hands to go up too quickly, thus restricting the arc. As a result, you are liable to come down on the ball with a chopping motion. George Duncan, a famous professional many years ago, always said that to hit the golf ball correctly you had to push the left arm out and up, and there is nothing to suggest that anyone has since found a better or a simpler method.

'if the swing is in a wide arc, the balance of weight will automatically go over to the right leg and foot'

Now that you have got the club up, what about balance? Many beginners become bemused by talk of weight transference. But if the swing is in a wide arc, the balance of weight will go over to the right leg and foot in a perfectly natural manner because you cannot push the club out and up without it doing so. And when it does, the left heel must come off the ground and this in itself puts the weight on the right foot. As the hips have turned, so have the shoulders and you are now in a position where your back is towards the direction in which you are to hit the ball. Providing, of course, the head has remained steady, you are still looking at the ball and the left shoulder is pointing to the ground—where it should be pointing.

And do not worry if all these things seem too many to remember. In practice, you do not think about them at all during the swing and, provided your grip is correct, a correct arc of swing and correct balance will follow as a matter of course.

So the clubhead has been taken up and you have turned as far as you can with comfort. The next thing is to bring it down in a smooth accelerating action so that it is moving at its maximum speed at the moment it makes contact with the ball. Some beginners take this to mean that in order to attain that maximum speed you have to pull the club down violently from the top. This is not so. What you have to do is to accelerate gradually on the downswing, starting quite slowly and without any semblance of a jerk. It should be remembered that those players who have a full backswing, ie, longer than many, do not have the same tendency to jerk the club down because they have more time in which to accelerate. How far one takes the club back is a matter for the individual. You will soon know when you have taken it too far back because the chances are you will have swayed away from the ball and so lost balance.

There has often been talk about 'the pause at the top', meaning that between taking the clubhead back and bringing it down there should be a pause. Some players do this, but in the main I feel it is a gimmick used to impress upon pupils that they should not hurry at the start of the downswing but should allow a split second to elapse before that transference of weight from the right leg to the left which is vital if you are to pull down the clubhead.

This transference is started by the hips and then, as they turn in the direction you intend the ball to travel, the hands pull down the clubhead at ever increasing speed. Simultaneously, the weight will go over to the outside of the left foot, and by this time the hands are starting to move so fast that they are in front of the clubhead. If they are not in front of the clubhead you will be hitting too early and the result will be a sloppy shot. While there must be no jerking down of the clubhead and while the downward stroke must start slowly, there must be nothing half-hearted about the actual bringing down of the clubhead. What is needed is a rapid building up of the speed so that when the moment comes for the club to hit the ball you can sweep it away.

'hitting against a firmly braced left side'

To achieve good results there must be perfect timing. If at the moment of impact the clubhead has passed its maximum speed much force will have been dissipated and, conversely, if it has not achieved maximum speed much potential force will fail to have been generated. Most beginners lose force when the ball is hit because they do not keep their arms straight. When the clubhead is coming down the position of the right elbow is important, and it should not be allowed to fly away from the body. The flying right elbow is a bad fault because it means that the hands are not able to bring down the clubhead keeping the face of the club square to the ball. If you keep the left arm straight and keep the right elbow close to the body on the downward swing you will not go far wrong because the left arm will be straight throughout. And when the moment of impact is reached, the right arm will also be straight and you will have the feeling that you are pressing both hands downwards.

By that time the left leg will be straight as well and you will be hitting against a firmly braced left side. Any bending of the left arm, and what is called a collapsed left side, will result in a bad shot. And the swing does not finish there because the hands must be carried right through after you have hit the ball. The left arm is still straight and the momentum of the stroke will carry the clubhead right through. During the whole movement of the swing the left shoulder lifts, sweeping the hands through and upwards.

One of the chief faults with beginners is that by failing to control hands and arms they tend to throw the clubhead away from them as they start the downswing. Then, realising that they are not going to hit the ball square in the back, they have to draw in their arms to make contact. I believe that this fault is more prevalent than the one of keeping *both* arms too close to the body throughout the entire swing.

Many people have written about the secret of the golf swing. There *is* no secret in it, but if there is one cardinal point to be remembered it is that the right elbow must not be allowed to fly all over the place. Almost equally important is to remember that if the ball is to be hit correctly the only place to hit it is square in the back.

Many famous teachers and golf professionals claim that golf is a simple game and though few ordinary players are likely to agree with that wholeheartedly, there is no doubt that many, perhaps most golfers, do make out the swing to be a more complicated matter than it really is. If the arc of the swing is wide—and that can only be attained by taking back the club-

'bringing it down with the right elbow close to your side'

head low, with a straight left arm and a right arm as straight as you can make it—then there is only one way the clubhead can be brought down, by drawing it in towards you at the top of the swing and bringing it down with the right elbow close to your side. Then you will hit the ball square in the back.

So forget most of the things you hear golfers talk about, too many of them are simply trying to correct one fault with another, forgetting that in golf, as in many other things in life, the simple way is usually the best way. Worse still, a lot of them have even forgotten what the simple way is.

The golf swing is one natural, co-ordinated movement. It is not a thing of bits and pieces. It is all over in a flash with no time in which to change the course of the swing unless in a frantic last-minute effort to get the clubhead right just before it strikes the ball. And by then it is usually too late. Co-ordinated and smooth, with the left arm straight and the right elbow well into the body—that, and hitting against a braced left side, pretty well sums up the points which go to make a good golf swing.

8. FROM THE TEE

Now we are out on the course and one thing to be made clear is that, no matter which club you are using, the swing is the same except for short approach shots, when it is shorter. Some golfers seem to have the idea that there is one swing for the woods and another for the irons, but that is quite wrong.

Having established that point, let us now turn to the teeshots. The object of playing a teeshot or driving, whichever you prefer to call it, is to send the ball as far as you can and also to steer it clear of trouble. This is easier said than done and all too often a beginner becomes petrified with nervousness as he walks on to the first tee or is too eager to try and hit the cover off the ball. In trying to do so, he swings far too quickly so that the whole timing of the stroke is ruined, the ball goes any old where, and one or more strokes are lost at the very start of the round.

There is an old American expression 'You drive for show and putt for dough', but it is not altogether correct. Certainly, you can often recover from bad teeshots but if you can play good ones it makes the game very much easier and increases one's confidence. It is important, therefore, that you step on to the tee in the right frame of mind, and that is a calm frame of mind. Not only do you want to hit the ball a reasonable distance but you must also know where you are going to hit it. If there is trouble on the right-hand side of the fairway, you aim for the clear, and though you may not always succeed in reaching it you must have confidence in what you are planning to do.

It is this matter of confidence, or lack of it, that contributes to fast swinging, for not only do many golfers try to hit the ball hard but they also want to get the stroke over with. This, in some measure, is because the driver has a longer shaft than any other club in the bag and to adopt a comfortable stance you have to be further away from the ball than with other clubs. Consequently many golfers feel that they do not have the same degree of control over the driver as they have with other clubs, but this is purely a psychological matter and if you have any such ideas, get them out of your head.

The first thing you do on starting a round of golf is to tee up the ball on the teepeg. When the faces of drivers were less deep than they are now, teepegs were pushed well into the ground, but nowadays this is not necessary and a good way of judging how far the teepeg should be pushed in is to place the first two fingers of one hand on the peg and with the thumb, press it down to the extent that you can withdraw your two fingers comfortably. This is only a guide, however, and individual golfers will have their own theories on the subject.

You then decide where you are to aim, and many beginners, happy to hit the ball at all, go wrong at this point. What you should try to do is to hit the ball into a position which will make the next shot as easy as possible. And remember that when playing from the tee, it is most important that the stroke should not be hurried. If it is, you will not be able to achieve the wide arc of the clubhead which goes to make a smooth action. The strange thing is that when you swing slowly with the driver— and this, indeed, goes for all clubs—you will find that you sweep the ball away so leisurely that you just don't feel that you have hit it at all. One thing that will help you to sweep the ball away is to make sure that you are are standing in a position where the ball is not too near the right heel. Most good golfers have it opposite the left heel, and certainly not further back than a line drawn from a point in the centre of the two feet. Generally speaking, the position of the ball should not be altered over-much for the different shots, but some licence can be taken when playing from the tee if one feels more comfortable that way. Certainly, having the ball nearer a line drawn from the left heel makes you stretch out that little bit and so helps you to follow-through in the manner prescribed in the previous chapter.

If you have the ball too far back, it will cramp your swing because you will not be able to get into the back of the ball without chopping down on it, and that is just what you must not do. With a chopping motion, the ball will either be hit on the top and go scurrying away into the rough on the left, or you will have to sway backwards to make contact and the chances are that the ball will then rise gently into the air and plop down only a few yards in front of you.

Remember that the clubhead must come into the back of the ball, and it must do so after a descent which has been gradual. Consider a man on a bowling green kneeling or bending when he delivers his bowl because he wants to sweep the hand holding the bowl as nearly parallel to the ground as he can. He does not bring his hand down and throw the bowl on to the grass, for if he did the bowl would not be sent on its way smoothly and would lose both pace and direction. Max Faulkner once referred to this similarity between golf and bowls and it well illustrates the point I am trying to make—that the clubhead must not come down in a steep descent but should be near the ground quite a few inches before it makes contact with the ball.

To return now to the question of timing, the act of hitting the ball when the clubhead is at its maximum speed. It is easy to talk and write about, but not so easy to put into practice. The truth of the matter is that perfect timing is something that comes only with experience, the experience gained by the correct use of the hands, the attainment of good balance and a relaxed outlook on the game. If the weight has been correctly trans-ferred from the right leg on the backswing to the left leg on the downswing, and the hands are pulled with ever increasing acceleration, then you have a chance to get proper timing into your stroke.

Many beginners at golf hear about this pulling down of the

hands and think that they must put all their energy into doing so from the very first moment of the downward swing. The result is that they lunge at the ball so that the clubhead is slowing down as it comes near the ball instead of being at its maximum speed, as it should be. This is called 'hitting from the top'.

The driver is a useful club in many ways. If you hit the ball correctly with it you will cover a lot of distance, which not only gives you a good send-off to the hole but also puts you into a confident frame of mind for the shots to follow. Bad driving, on the other hand, can get you into all sorts of trouble and play havoc with your confidence. So relax, don't allow yourself to be hurried into a lunging stroke but bring the clubhead down fast enough to sweep the ball away in one smooth flowing movement.

9. THE FAIRWAY WOODS

Before playing a wood from the fairway the first thing is to consider how the ball is lying. If it is lying close, that is on something of a bare patch, or if it is in a hollow, the chances are that it is not a lie for a wooden club at all. If it is lying reasonably well, the next question is which wooden club to use.

It may be that you have in your bag a No 2 wood, which has an almost straight face with only a little more loft than a driver. If so, you would be well advised to keep it in your bag until you have become more proficient at the game, as it is a difficult club for beginners to handle and not one with which to experiment. Better to concentrate instead on the No 3 or No 4 wood as the greater degree of loft on the faces of these two clubs makes it easier to get the ball up in the air, which is essential if you are to get distance. The shafts of the No 3 and No 4 woods are also slightly shorter than that of the No 2 wood and this, in some peculiar way, seems to give beginners more confidence.

It was noted in the previous chapter that, when playing the driver, some golfers have the ball opposite the left heel. For playing the fairway woods, however, this position would be wrong and the ball should be towards the centre of the feet.

Since the object when playing the fairway woods is to get distance, you would not use such a club if you felt you could reach the green with an iron—for the simple reason that if you hit the ball well with the wood it would surely go soaring over the green. Or take the case of an inexperienced golfer who is, say, two hundred yards from the green with the wind in his favour. He thinks to himself: 'Now if I hit a really good wooden club shot I might get to the green'. What has not registered in his mind's eye is a couple of bunkers just in front of the green. And you will have already guessed where he puts the ball.

A similar lack of judgement is shown by a player who, thinking he can clear a row of bunkers, finds himself trapped by them when, if he had played short of the bunkers with an iron club, he would have been quite safe and able to chip over them to the green with his next shot. An example, this, of why people are so fond of saying that golf has to be played with the head.

No less important than knowing when to play a wooden club is to know which particular one to use in the circumstances, and it will be helpful in deciding the latter question to remember that the No 3 wood sends the ball further than the No 4.

The grip, the stance and the swing for wooden clubs played off the fairway are exactly the same as in the swing for the driver. There are those who insist that it is not the same and that bringing the clubhead down on a steeper angle than with the driver helps to get the ball into the air. What those who cherish this theory forget is that the loft of the club will get the ball into the air. It has also been said that with the fairway woods the ball should be hit more on the upstroke than it is with the driver. But in playing fairway woods, how can there be time as the clubhead is coming into the ball to decide whether it is to be hit more on the upstroke? To accelerate the hands on the downswing until they have built up to maximum speed at the moment of impact is all one can do and the loft of the club-face can be relied upon to get the ball into the air. So forget anything you have heard or read about any difference between the swing of a fairway wood and a driver—it is just another of those unfounded theories with which some people like to complicate the game.

Fairway woods, particularly the No 3 or No 4—some people even use a No 5—are clubs with which you soon feel comfortable and confident once you have become accustomed to them. And to become accustomed to them, the first thing a novice has to remember is to play them only from good lies where the grass is lush, or reasonably so. To try to nip the ball up from a hard lie is very difficult for beginners and those who have had no lessons, or only a few, would be well advised to limit themselves at first to hitting the ball with a No 5 iron. This will help them to get the feel of the clubs, so to speak, and is a point to be stressed because so many books take it for granted that all golfers will have started off with dozens of lessons whereas, in fact, this is true in comparatively few cases.

So first make sure you are capable of getting the ball into the air with perhaps a lofted iron and then, when you come to experiment with fairway woods, I predict that you will take to them like a duck to water. But if you start off by using them for every shot on the fairway, even from a bad lie, you will become discouraged because you will probably be snatching at the ball with a quick and over-steep swing, thinking 'This shot is going to be hard. I must get the ball up quickly.'

Which is quite the wrong frame of mind, of course, quite apart from the fact that you should not be playing a wood off a hard lie anyway, and that the stroke should never be hurried either with fairway woods or any other clubs.

If you go to big golf tournaments and can get close enough to the golf stars you will be amazed to see them using wooden clubs from bad lies in the rough. This they are able to do because of their great strength, high degree of skill, and tough experience. It is the dream of almost every golfer to be able to play woods from long grass or from a bad lie in the rough, but until you have accumulated a great deal of experience it would be as well not to try to realise that dream. True, there will be times when you are tempted to use a No 3 or No 4 wood from long grass, because the ball is lying up on a tuft. But do not be misled by this because the chances are that, unless you are very accurate, the clubhead will go underneath the ball, which will hardly move at all.

So, keep your woods for shots from the fairway, at least until you have mastered them. And you will master them if you have plenty of confidence, swing leisurely in a wide arc and sweep through the ball.

10. THE LONG AND MEDIUM IRONS

For those who do not indulge in the luxury of a full range of clubs right at the start, the irons they are likely to find most use for will be the No 3 iron, the No 5, the No 7 and a 9 iron, or some kind of deep-faced club with which to get out of trouble. The No 3 would be for the longer shots, the others for progressively shorter ones. We noted in an earlier chapter that as the numbers of clubs increase so does the loft on the face, and the greater the loft the higher the ball will be put into the air with, naturally, a consequent loss of distance. It may be that you have other irons in the bag, but the principle is still the same, and, theoretically at least, the difference in distance which the respective irons will drive the ball is about fifteen yards. In other words, the ball when hit with a No 5 iron will travel, in theory, some fifteen yards less than a ball played with a No 4 iron. To find out how far you can hit an average length with any iron, or with any other club for that matter, go out on the practice ground and measure the distance you hit shots by means of some landmark, or if there is no landmark pace out, say, 150 yards and 200 yards etc, placing something down on the grass. To find your average with each club will give you a rough idea of what lies within your capabilities and enable you to make some kind of plan of campaign. There will be more on this in the chapter dealing with practice.

In deciding which iron club to play, two factors have to be taken into account. One is the distance you want, or hope to hit the ball, the other is how the ball is lying. If the lie is good and the distance right for, say, a No 3 iron, then that will be the club to use. Obviously, if the lie is not good then you will be forced to play, say, a No 5 or a No 7 iron for safety's sake. There is no point in taking a No 3 iron and scuttling the ball along the ground into a bunker, so use your judgement and remember that the old maxim, 'better safe than sorry' applies equally to golf.

There are few more pleasing experiences in golf than to send a long iron shot seering down the fairway with the ball clear of trouble and perhaps landing on the green. And if it is a well-hit No 3 iron into the wind, that is even more satisfying. Many golfers, however, having become attached to their No 3 or No 4 woods, prefer to play them rather than a No 3 iron, and indeed there is not a great deal of difference between the distance one can send the ball with either club. Even so, it is not what might be called orthodox golf and whereas you can play the iron off a close lie, a wooden club shot from the same lie might well end in disaster. Once again, it is a matter of good judgement and of gaining experience of what each club can do and when you should play it.

The following table will give you some idea of the distances you should be able to hit iron shots, providing everything goes well. It can only be a guide and if you are just starting to play golf you may think you will never be able to hit the ball anything like these distances. Do not be discouraged, you soon will be able to do so.

Here, then, is the table:

No 2 iron	180 yards
No 3 iron	165 yards
No 4 iron	150 yards
No 5 iron	135 yards
No 6 iron	125 yards
No 7 iron	120 yards
No 8 iron	110 yards

Star players can, of course, hit the ball much further but these are fair averages for more ordinary mortals, and take into account the fact that not every shot is a perfect one. I look on it like this. If you hit a drive 200 yards long and then hit two No 5 iron shots 135 yards each, keeping well out of trouble, your ball will have covered a distance of 470 yards, which is the length of a long par four hole. If you have actually reached the green and sunk the ball in two putts then, with the stroke you would get from your handicap, you would have played the hole in par, which corresponds to perfect golf. It is all theoretical, of course, but is the ideal to keep in mind.

I have referred to sweeping the ball away with the irons, even though there are some experts who disagree about this. Max Faulkner, for example, says 'yes', whereas others, like the great American professional, Doug Ford, say 'no'. I am inclined to agree with Ford for the simple reason that, the faces of all the irons having a certain amount of loft, you can hit down on the ball with the assurance that the loft will make the ball rise into the air. And, remember, the swing for all the irons except the very short ones is just the same as it is for the woods. It is the loft of the club which makes the ball get into the air and not your swing.

What is important is balance. If this is correct you will be pulling down the clubhead, and so long as your left shoulder is not coming up too quickly there is nothing to worry about. Do not get into the habit of so many golfers of fussing about every little thing one should or should not do. The swing takes only a split second and if it is to be effective it must become an automatic action.

One point which confuses many golfers of moderate ability is the taking of a divot. When they go to a professional tournament they see the stars playing an iron shot and when they have played it a great piece of turf, a 'divot', flies through the air. This happens because they go down and through the ball with such force (often with a steeper swing than one would recommend for beginners) that they carve the turf from its place after they have hit the ball, not before they have hit it. You would be well advised to forget about this taking a divot at the early stage of your golfing life because you will not be able to hit the ball hard enough anyway. Besides, there are some tournament professionals who, as I have suggested, place more reliance on sweeping the ball away rather than hitting it away, and so have rarely taken a divot in their lives. Divots, like expensive food dishes, are only for those who can afford them. And golf beginners, or even those who have played for some time, cannot afford the luxury. They have too many other things on their plate. You will be able to take divots all in good time, though when you become a first-class player it is most unlikely that you will be making any effort to do so intentionally.

Now there is the question of stance for the long and medium irons. The ball should rest equally between the two feet and, of course, you will be standing nearer the ball than you would with the wooden clubs because of the shorter shafts. For the same reason the stance will be a little narrower than for the woods. But you must stand in the same comfortable way with the knees slightly bent and no tension apparent anywhere. Should the stance be open (left foot drawn back), square (both toes square to the line of flight of the ball), or should it be closed (the left foot pushed forward)? This is a subject we have already touched upon and one could quote many authoritative books which variously advocate each one of the three.

My own feeling is that a very open stance tends to make some golfers pull in their arms on the downward stroke, with the result that to get into position to make contact with the ball, they come across it. So I go for a square stance as being the safest for the majority. As for the long irons, the arc of the swing has to be wide as it is for the woods. In fact, the arc should be as wide as you can make it for the medium irons as well, but as their shafts are shorter it will obviously not be as wide as for the longer clubs. But that does not mean to say that the arms should bend all over the place. The clubhead should be taken back low to the ground, the weight put on the right foot and then, as the hands are taken up, the hips and shoulders will turn as a matter of course.

Some beginners seem to think that if their body turns they will lose control of the situation, but this will not happen if they keep their head steady and their chin tucked into the left shoulder. If the head is not steady and the left shoulder is not pointing to the ground, then you can be sure that you have started to sway away from the ball—a fatal mistake when playing a golf shot. The feet, too, must be anchored, albeit the weight goes on the right foot on the upswing and then is transferred to the left on the downswing.

One of the worst faults when playing iron shots is to hurry them. Most novices at the game are afraid of a swing they think is slow—but which is almost certainly much quicker than they think—because they fear that the ball will not go into the air. There should be no fears about that. If the left side is firm and the arms are straight as the clubhead strikes the ball and continues towards the line of flight, then the ball will go away in the direction that was intended.

An old professional, Charles Macey, who was for years at the Crowborough Beacon Club in Sussex, used to teach his pupils to swing to a record of the Blue Danube waltz. ONE, two, three, ONE, two, three, ONE, two, three. Just hum the tune to yourself to get the rhythm as you swing a golf club and you will soon see that it does help to establish a flowing movement. That is if you say the first 'one' at the top of the backswing, and every second 'one' when the clubhead is in the same position. And for those who are not old enough to know the great tune, let me add that it is in three-quarter time with the accent on the first beat. It may sound crazy, but just try it out and you may well change your mind.

If you have trouble playing the longer irons in your bag, give them a rest and concentrate on the medium ones with their more lofted faces. That will give you confidence. And the grip for the irons is the same as for the woods, about an inch down from the end of the shaft (that part which is nearest to your body), or perhaps a little lower if you feel more confident that way.

In time, as your experience grows, you will find that you can become very accurate with the long and medium irons, always assuming, of course, that you hit the ball with the middle of the blade of the club. If you hit it nearer the neck (where the shaft joins the head) or nearer the toe, then you are in for trouble. That is why the swing is so important.

One other aspect of iron play not yet touched upon is that of iron shots from the tee at short holes. One is accustomed to seeing professionals throwing down the ball on the tee at a short hole and banging it away. For the ordinary player, however, it is best that the ball should be on a peg, but not teed up high. You will then be sure of getting the height which is essential, as there is usually much trouble to be found between tee and green at a short hole. The shot should be played as one would play an iron shot from the fairway.

11.   THE SHORT IRONS

Apart from the kind of shots for which they are primarily designed the short irons can be used out of context, so to speak. They are, for instance, invaluable for playing recovery shots, while the No 5 iron can be used for all manner of little shots and can rightly be termed a 'maid of all work'.

But let us start with the shots for which the short irons were intended, beginning with the No 5 iron. Some might call this a medium iron but I prefer to put it into the short iron category because it can so often be used for shorter and less lofted shots.

The stance for the irons becomes only a little less wide as their numbers increase. Remember that the shafts are also becoming progressively shorter, so that to be comfortable the stance has to be narrower and you are also nearer the ball. The ball should still be halfway between the feet, and there should be no difference between the length of the swing for the short irons and that for the medium irons, because it is bad for beginners to overswing with any club. The only time the swing should be very short is for a tiny shot.

By the time you are thinking of taking a No 5 iron out of your bag, even if you are a beginner, you are either within striking distance of the green or proposing to use it for a recovery shot. In the former case, you have to be sure that the No 5 is the right club to play to reach the green and then, having decided that it is, be prepared to hit the ball boldly. As a rule, there is less trouble immediately behind a green than there is in front of or at the sides, so it pays to be bold. You will find the No 5 iron a most rewarding club and at first you will most probably be using it a great deal more often than any other club.

To be able to hit a crisp shot with the short irons you need a good springboard, so pressing the hands forward (ie, to the left) prior to hitting the ball is essential. And do not forget the little waggles of the club which go with this 'forward press'. These are not just for show but help to settle you for the shot and give momentum to the swing.

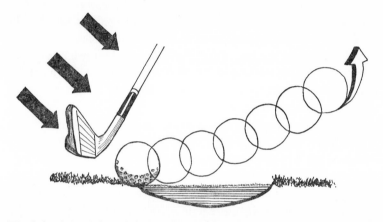

'The loft of the club and the downward blow with which the ball is struck are sufficient to get the ball into the air'

You may not have a No 6 iron in your bag when you first start playing golf, but if you have it is played just like a No 5 iron though the ball will not go so far. So to the No 7 iron. Again, this is a most versatile club which can be used for a variety of purposes—its traditional one and also for playing little chip shots and recovery shots. As the loft of the irons is now becoming more pronounced the No 7 can be used for playing over hazards, and also when the ball is lying on a bare patch of ground. And here those who have not had a great deal of experience sometimes run into difficulties. With the loft of the face in mind, they think that the ball has to be scooped up and this results in a fluffed shot. Perhaps this tendency is more often evident with the No 8 iron or the No 9 iron but it is also present when playing the No 7. So please get this scooping business out of your head from the outset. It just doesn't work. The loft of the club and the downward blow with which the ball is struck are quite sufficient to get the ball in the air. This cannot be too strongly emphasised.

And now to say something about spin, which is not such a technical matter as it may sound. In table tennis backspin is a valuable asset and to impart it you chop the ball down so that the bat makes contact with the back of the ball. If you hit the ball in a straighforward manner with what might be called a low level stroke the ball will fly lower and when it lands on the other side of the net it will fly off the table in a low trajectory. But if you have chopped it, the ball will stand up when it lands and spin back towards you.

I am not now advocating a downward chopping action with a golf club, but the clubhead does have to come down from a height and, without consciously altering the swing into a very steep one, the loft on the club will impart spin providing the club has made contact with the back of the ball without first hitting the ground. In table tennis you have to chop down on the ball because there is no loft on a table tennis bat whereas, in golf, the clubhead striking the ball at the right time in the right place is enough to get the ball into the air and with backspin. One could call it striking the ball with a sharp descending blow. But there must be no scooping of the ball. That is fatal.

'Ah', but you may say, 'I often strike the ball correctly, yet it lands on the green and then runs and runs until it is over the back.' The short answer to that is that the ball has not been struck with a descending blow. The No 7 iron, or whatever, has not 'skinned' the outside of the ball but has scraped the grass just before hitting the ball, and maybe, too, the stroke was too leisurely from start to finish, which is not good. Acceleration on the downward stroke is just as vital for the shorter clubs as it is for the longer ones.

To move on to the more lofted irons, the No 8 and the No 9, these you will be using mainly for recovery shots and for playing over hazards, so there is not much that needs saying about them for the time being. Again the swing is the same, except when playing the very little shots the feet are closer together and you stand nearer the ball, the latter because the shafts are shorter and closer proximity to the ball gives you greater control over the shot. I think also that the stance should be more open, ie, that the left foot should be drawn back from the direction in which you want the ball to go.

Many beginners are nervous of playing a full No 8 iron shot, which might be in the region of 100 yards or a little more and, if there is nothing in the way, prefer to play a more gentle shot with a No 7 iron. There is nothing very wrong with this, but the degree of force with which you must hit the ball does call for a considerable amount of judgement. Remember that, with such a shot, the ball will run on after it lands, and this running-on business is something which many golfers can never prevent all their golfing lives. If they played full shots with more lofted irons more often they would eventually learn to play the ball with backspin, employing the method mentioned earlier.

Pitch and run shots—where the ball goes off on a low trajectory and then runs on after it lands—have their uses, nonetheless, but they can only be played with any assurance of success when you are near the green. To play a low trajectory shot any real distance from the green is to take something of a chance, even though such shots can often be brought off successfully.

In the early days of golf, the Old Timers were very good at half shots, pitch and runs and the like, but that was largely because the limited selection of clubs then available made it necessary for them to more or less invent shots at which they often became expert. Today there is a club for every specific job and improvisation is less necessary, though it still can be usefully employed sometimes, as when playing from a bush or from underneath or around the branches of a tree. But though improvisation can occasionally get you out of tight corners in golf, it will not make you a great player, and you will get a far better start to the game if you utilise all the clubs you have to their best advantage (even if you have your favourite) and that means using them for the shots for which they were primarily intended.

Many golfers, and not only those new at the game, find the short irons difficult to play, and when I have played bad shots with them it was usually because I was allowing the right hand to take control. I have never discovered why this should have been so, except, perhaps, that a little anxiety may have been creeping into my game and in trying to punch the ball away in a hurry I thought, quite wrongly, that a tighter grip with the right hand would help.

My cure, and it was entirely a home-made one, was to grip extra tightly with the left hand until things got back to normal again. Some of my professional friends have laughed at this 'cure' but all I can say is that it worked for me, especially with the more lofted irons such as the No 8 and No 9. At least I stopped fluffing the ball and even if I could not be sure of getting the ball near the hole every time, I was able to get it on to the green, which is better than plopping it up a few yards in front of you or scuttling it along the ground.

12. THE APPROACH SHOTS

It is not easy to differentiate between the short irons and approach shots, because all shots except recovery ones played by the short irons are approach shots, the intention being to put the ball on the green and make it stay there. But the clubs generally used for approach shots are the very lofted irons, except when the player has decided to play a pitch and run shot as described in the previous chapter, or a run-up shot where the ball never leaves the ground. The dangers of such shots when played from quite a long distance from the green have already been mentioned but nearer the green they can be employed with a greater chance of success. For such shots a No 5 or a No 7 iron can be used from just off the green, though some players, including many professionals, prefer the 'Texas wedge', which was mentioned in Chapter Two. Most ordinary golfers, however, find it a difficult club to play and have to employ other methods.

The first thing to do when you are about to play a short shot to the green is to weigh up the situation. How far are you from the hole? Is the ball lying well? Are there any hazards to be got over? Is the pin near the front of the green, leaving you very little room to play over a bunker (if there is one), or is it in the centre of the green allowing you some latitude? Having deliberated these points, you have then to make up your mind which club you are going to use and what type of shot you are going to play.

The distance your ball is from the green is of great importance, and if you are some distance away the club to use is probably a No 8 iron. It may be, if you have a No 9 iron in your bag, that you will be tempted to play it, but remember that beginners, when they are trying to be particularly accurate, are apt to become nervous so that they spare the shot, with the result that the ball stops short of the green. There is, therefore, much to be said for using a club that will get you there without forcing.

For the short approach shots, the stance should be narrower than for any other shots which have to be played in golf, because for these it is not necessary to take a full swing at the club.

And though all along in this book I have been advising a square stance, for little shots to the green the stance can be open. The reason for this is because with an open stance—that is one with the left foot drawn back from the intended line of flight—the left side is out of the way, and that means that the swing is more upright than it is for long shots. But please don't try to make it so—it will happen as a matter of course. The more upright swing will bring the clubhead down at a steeper angle, and if the club hits down on the back of the ball then you will have backspin on the ball.

But do not chop down at the ball intentionally. The swing is still a smooth, one-piece action. And do not be confused by what has been said earlier about a wide arc to the swing. Basically, the arc of the swing is the same for all shots.

Now for the different types of short shots. There are really only two in regular use, the pitch and the pitch and run. Pitching to the green is used when there are obstacles in the way. It would be madness in such circumstances to play any shot other than one in which the ball is put high in the air. Another reason for playing a high-flying shot to the green is when the green is sloping down to the back. Then a pitch and run shot would land on the green and the ball would run down the slope. That is the difference between a pitch and a pitch and run shot. In the first, the ball should bounce once or twice and then stop (even spin back if it has been correctly played). In the second, the ball will strike the green and then run on until lack of momentum brings it to a halt.

The club to use for a pitch is the No 9 iron—a wedge is even better for those who possess one and have learnt how to use it. If you do not have a No 9 iron then a No 8 will have to suffice. The stance should be open and you should grip the club a little

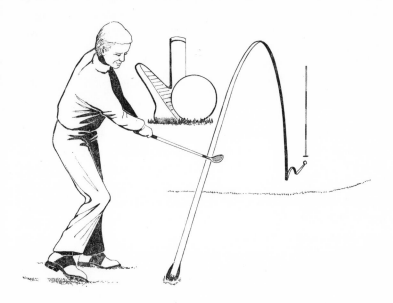

Pitch shot played with a wedge or No 9 iron

way down the shaft, perhaps as much as two inches. Don't spare the shot; in other words, come down on the back of the ball with a crisp blow and aim for the pin. Don't play a pitch shot to land on the ground in front of the green. The pin should be the target, but remember that the ball will run on a little after it lands, certainly if you are using a No 8 iron and to a lesser extent with a No 9. Wedge shots properly played cause the ball to stop immediately, or almost immediately.

The other shot, the pitch and run, should be used when there is a clear road in to the flag. The No 8 iron is the club to play, but if you are a little further away then the No 7 can be used.

By 'further away' I mean a distance of about 30 yards, though the pitch and run can be played from just off the green. It is then commonly referred to as a chip shot and can be played with any club down to a No 5 iron. With the pitch and run and the chip shot, the ball should be made to land some distance from the pin—about halfway would be just about right. For the longer pitch and run, try to make the ball land just in front of the green.

Pitch and run shot played with a No 5 iron

In selecting the spot on which you are hoping to make the ball hit the turf, any slight undulation in the ground must be taken into consideration. If, for instance, there is a small bump, it would be silly to try to make the ball land on the upward slope, rather should you make it land on the down slope. Also to be considered is the fact that the ball will move off the slope at a quicker pace. So if the bump is fairly high, you would not use the pitch and run at all, but a pitch.

The pitch and run is altogether a more gentle shot than the pitch. The stance should be square, or just very slightly open, because as no backspin is required the ball does not need to be hit with the club coming down at such a steep angle as for the pitch. For little pitch and run shots the weight should be on the left foot. The arms should be allowed to swing freely but without any intentional bending of the wrists. In fact, the little chip shot can be likened to a miniature long iron shot in some respects, certainly inasmuch as you chip the ball away with a smooth action.

The club is not taken back far but it should be taken back low and kept low after the ball has been struck. And don't worry about the ball not lifting from the ground. The loft of the club will do that as a matter of course.

A variation of the pitch and run is what might be called the run-up shot, which is played mostly on seaside courses where the ball runs more predictably—or should I say 'runs on' more predictably—than on inland courses. With this type of shot, played when there is no obstacle between the ball and the flag, the ball is run along the ground usually with a No 5 iron. The secret of the shot is in correctly judging the strength to give it. Unless you all but miss the ball you can be sure that it is going on to the green. What you are really trying to do is to get the ball very close to the flag, perhaps even to get it into the hole. So do not spare the shot but hit it strongly enough for the ball to be up alongside the hole. In putting there is an old saying: 'Never up, never in.' and this also applies to the little run-up shots.

The run-up shot is not often used by the experts, who rely for the most part on the pitch and run, but for those who are less accomplished it is, at the very least, a safe shot. Some crafty, experienced old golfers can play this shot quite a distance from the green with good results, but the novice would be wise to reserve it for distances of just a few yards to start with. It might well be that you could get on the green with this kind of shot from quite a distance but you might not get the ball near the flag. And the very fact that you have obviously missed the green with the previous shot suggests that you are in some kind of difficulty and now badly need to get the ball near the hole and then down in a single putt. Moreover, during the novice stage, many a shot intended to be a pitch is apt to end by running along the ground.

Although the run-up is just a little shot, do not make the mistake of playing it loosely. The grip of the club must be firm. You must, as always, look closely at the ball and you must hit it a crisp little blow with the clubhead going back only a short way and following through only a short way. The hands can be a couple of inches or so from the end of the club.

There is another club besides a No 4 or a No 5 iron which can be used for little shots just off the green—the putter. If the ground between the ball and the hole is perfectly smooth and has only the smallest of undulations, some players prefer not to risk putting the ball into the air for even a fraction of an inch, which must happen with any club other than a putter, when the ball can be kept on the ground from the moment it is struck. So they use a putter, striking the ball a good solid blow to send it the required distance. As I have indicated previously this is a safe shot and can be a very telling one, though some experienced golfers tend to look upon it as a coward's shot. This would not worry me if I thought I could get near the flag by using it, any more than I would worry if my partner were playing a No 5 iron on the fairway and I, because I could not get the distance, was using a No 3 wood. A great thing in golf is to be aware of one's own capabilities, so if you feel more capable of getting the ball near the hole with a putter from off the green rather than with a No 5 or a No 7 iron then use the putter.

13. ON THE PUTTING GREEN

Putting is the most talked about department of the game. And it is the most talked about because it is not only the most important but also the most frustrating. A golfer may be very powerful from the tee, accurate with his fairway shots and adequate in his approach shots, but if he—or it can be she—is not a good holer-out then much of the good work which has gone before will have been wasted. Conversely, a player can have a bad drive, a good recovery shot, a useful fairway shot, a moderate approach, and then hole out in a single putt with the same final score at the hole as the golfer who has had three good shots and then taken two putts. In fact, the good player might even take three putts and the other will have won the hole in five to six. To hole a long putt is invaluable and to miss a short putt is disastrous.

Almost from the first day that golf was played many, many people have claimed to have discovered the 'secret' of putting. There is no secret. The best any golfer can do is to find a safe method of putting and stick to it. Naturally, there will always be golfers who are better at putting than others for a variety of reasons other than having a good method. For instance some find it hard, even impossible to judge distance accurately, others find it impossible to 'read' the greens. That means to judge whether the greens are fast or slow—to note whether they have been cut recently or whether they are dry and hard or soft and wet, or whether the path to the hole is straight or whether there are any slopes on the green. All one can do is to learn by experience.

Putting is not something that has any special mystique about it. Like other departments of golf, it is very much a question of commonsense aided by a calm outlook. The trouble with many golfers is that when they reach the green they become tensed up and anxious, especially if some bad shots have gone before and the player is over-anxious to make up for them. Or it may be that a particular putt has to be holed to win a hole or to save the match. That is when tension builds up, which is just another name for nervousness, no matter what anybody says.

Almost half the shots played on a golf course, other than by beginners, are played on the greens and bad putting is by no means exclusive to poor golfers. Professionals frequently three putt in tournaments and have even been known to take four putts. In the latter case it is probably because the player concerned lost his temper and became frustrated or careless—which is not to be recommended whether you are a beginner or an expert.

In my experience the best putters are golfers who have been long at the game and have perfected a system of putting which they have used consistently. The passing of the years has also made them concentrate on good putting to compensate for the loss of distance in the long shots which inevitably comes as one grows older.

This lesson was driven home to me very early in my golfing life by an elderly gentleman I played with many times. He had a half swing and nudged rather than hit the ball up the fairway. I don't suppose any shot went more than 150 yards, but he was rarely in trouble and invariably reached the green in three at medium or fairly long holes. He must have three putted occasionally but what I remember of his work on the greens was that his approach shot was very often near the flag and that he frequently holed out in one putt.

The very first thing in putting is to decide which is the right kind of putter for you. There are, as I previously mentioned, two different kinds, a centre-shafted putter, so called because the shaft joins the head on top of the centre of the blade, and the blade putter, which has the shaft joined to the head at the end of the blade. There are some variations but these are the two main types. You can only find out which is the one for you by trying out different putters on the practice putting green which most golf clubs possess, listening to the advice of a golf professional, and finally choosing the putter with which you feel comfortable and happy.

If a putter has served you well and then suddenly loses its magic, it is advisable to have a long hard think before swapping with another golfer or rushing out to buy another. A little calm thought may lead you to the conclusion that your putter—any putter—only does what it is directed to do and, that being so, it must be you, the controller of the putter, who is at fault.

The first thing to do on reaching the green and finding your ball on the putting surface is to gauge its distance from the hole, whether the ground slopes downwards or upwards to the hole, or whether the green slopes sideways. If the green is sloping downwards then obviously the ball has not to be struck too hard, if there is an upward slope then it has to be hit harder, and if there is a slope you will have to play to one side or another to allow the ball to turn in with the fall of the ground. There are also the questions of whether the green is dry or hard, and whether the grass is rather long or short. This all comes into the department of 'reading the green' but is really nothing more than a matter of commonsense.

If after you have looked at your ball and the hole you are still in some doubt, it is a good thing to look at the distance from the side, as from the apex of a triangle. And if you are not sure of the sideways slopes or the 'borrow', then go to the back of the hole and look at the ball from that angle. But try not to take too long about it otherwise your partner and other players may well become fractious. Slow play is something that is frowned upon by all but a few golfers, and this applies to all shots, not only to putts!

Putting is the most individual part of golf and so on any golf course, any day, you will see golfers of all shapes and sizes standing in every conceivable position trying to get the ball into the hole by all kinds of methods. Many of them, although they look rather odd, may well have discovered a way which works for them and are best left to it. Here I can only suggest a safe method of putting which has worked for thousands of golfers and which should work for you, unless you have already discovered another which serves you well.

First the grip. There is no one grip which might be termed standard and most golfers use the same overlapping grip they use for other shots, indeed whether or not they use it for other shots. Then, again, many players use the overlapping grip but have the forefinger of the right hand down the right side of the shaft—behind the shaft, really. This variation of the overlapping grip does give steadiness to the stroke, but it is mostly used by those middle-aged golfers who have been having putting troubles. The 'after forty finger' it has been called.

Another popular grip is called the 'reverse overlapping grip.' In this the index finger of the left hand overlaps the little finger of the right hand—some say it should overlap two fingers— and it is claimed that this grip gives added steadiness to the stroke. Some golfers who have been in dire trouble on the greens actually putt with the left hand below the right, but this is not a practice to be recommended.

The main thing about the grip—and I would recommend the ordinary overlapping grip—is that it should be comfortable. It should not be tense but the fingers must be in control because they are sensitive and putting is a delicate operation.

It is the stance perhaps, which has the greatest variations. Some play with a slightly closed stance (the left foot pushed forward), an open stance (the left foot drawn back) or a square stance (both feet in line to the direction you hope to hit the ball being the guide). My own preference is for the square stance, on the grounds that if you start playing about with the position of the feet in the absence of a guide line you are liable to get into trouble. Your head should be over the ball, which is easier to do if you use the square stance, and the ball should

be just a few inches inside the left foot. The feet should only be
slightly apart, so that you are fairly upright and not crouching.
You will see many people crouching when putting, but then
you see many people hitting the ball into the trees or the rough,
and there is no sense in following a bad example.

The 'after forty finger'

Now we come to that part of the putting stroke which perhaps
causes more controversy than any other—whether the ball should
be tapped with a quick movement of the wrists, or whether

it should be sent in the direction of the hole with one smooth movement of the hands. The difference between the two methods is that with a tap of the ball you bend the wrists, whereas when you stroke the ball you do not bend the wrists. Many golfers use a combination of the two methods, but to avoid confusion we will go for the method I consider the safest, because by stroking the ball less is likely to go wrong with it. If you are a wristy putter you are liable to turn the wrists and open or close the face of the club, which means that the ball will go off line.

In stroking the ball, the movement has to come from the shoulders and the arms should be straight but not tensed, while the knees should be slightly flexed to make you comfortable. The putter should be taken back quite a long way, but kept close to the grass. It should be taken straight back, and it will be taken straight back if your stance is square. If your stance is closed then it will almost certainly be taken back on the inside, and you will need to be a very good and experienced putter to use a closed stance.

After the putter has been taken back, then, with a one-piece shoulder and arms movement it is brought in behind the ball with the putter carrying on for only a very short way after the ball has been hit. It is not a good thing to follow-through too far, because when you hit the ball you have this in mind and there is a chance that the blade of the putter will be moving upwards. When that happens the ball will be hit with the bottom, or near the bottom, of the blade and the ball will not go as far as intended and will stop short of the hole. This often has a psychological effect on the player who, determined not to be short next time, sends the ball flying past the hole. And with the follow-through style of putting the ball is often hit too hard, so that it goes yards past the hole, leaving a nasty return putt which any golfer will tell you always seems difficult to hole.

Stroking the ball with one co-ordinated movement is not an infallible method of putting—none is—but it is a safe method and, all things being equal, it will work satisfactorily if you keep your wits about you. And keeping your wits about you is an essential part of getting the ball into the hole.

Loose arm movements and loose wrist movements are a fault displayed by many who have just taken up golf. It shows in the long game in the bending of elbows and the accentuated bending of the wrists, as if the players were scared of letting their arms do the work. Yet the arms cannot achieve their full power or accuracy if they are bent. In putting it has to be said that some golfers with both elbows bent can still achieve a one-piece movement and if they feel more comfortable that way, well and good, but in the long run I am convinced that having the arms straight makes for greater accuracy.

Some beginners at golf may find they are quite good putters, no matter which method they employ, but they will be in the minority for, as a general rule, good putting is something which comes only from experience and constant practice. Any keen golfer, however limited his playing time, should be able to afford the odd half hour practising putting and if there is any 'secret' in putting I would say that it is plenty of practice.

The reply to this from some people might be: 'But I have spent hours on the putting green and can putt well, yet when I go out on the course I don't get anything like the same results.' This may well be so, which brings us back to the old problem of tension or nervousness, call it what you will, and only the individual can cope with this. It will help to relax him if he tries to forget any upsetting shots which have gone before or what he has yet to do to win the game, and does not worry too much about the consequences of missing a short putt. Some golfers have even been known to consult psychiatrists in an attempt to cure their putting troubles, but this would seem to be taking what is, after all, a game, far too seriously.

14. TROUBLE SHOTS

Though a central theme of this book is that the swing is the same when playing all shots (other than a few exceptions such as little shots to the green) there will always be occasions when one must be prepared to compromise in order to retrieve a difficult situation, 'to get out of jail' golfers call it. Some famous golfers are so expert in playing recovery shots (even the best golfers get into trouble) that they are known as 'great scramblers'. This may often be said disparagingly, but the truth is that, recognising they are going to be faced with many awkward situations, these experts have made it their business to know just how to get out of them with the least possible penalty. And that in five words means 'Get back to the fairway'.

So when the ball goes flying off into the rough, play it cool and keep your head. If the ball is lying reasonably well, there will be a temptation to take a wood or a long iron in an effort to get distance and make up for the ground which has been lost. But think twice before having a slash at the ball with a big club, and don't play such a club unless you are sure you are going to get the ball clear of trouble. Far better, indeed, to use a lofted iron and get the ball back into play where it should have been in the first place, on the fairway.

If the ball is lying cleanly, there is no great trouble in playing out with a fairly lofted iron. You just play it as you would play the same iron on the fairway, but you must hit the ball accurately for if the club hits the grass behind the ball you will not move it very far. However, you can get the ball away from a good lie in the rough if you take care.

With long grass it is a very different story and a certain amount of improvisation is needed, even though it runs counter to what I have been advocating, taking the club back low and bringing it down in a wide arc. Because the grass behind the ball is long this is just not possible, so obviously you have to adopt different tactics.

To start with, you should be standing in front of the ball so that it is opposite the right toe. You then take the club up steeply and bring it down to strike the ball cleanly, much in the same way as you would strike it when playing a pitch shot. The club to use is a No 8 or a No 9 iron, and you must try to get the ball out to the nearest point of the fairway. The face of the club for this shot should be slightly closed, that is the point should be more forward, or to the left, than the heel of the club.

Many new golfers try to lift the ball out—to scoop it out, if you like—but the danger here is that the club will go right underneath the ball without removing it from its position. So always remember that scooping up the ball should never be attempted, whether from the fairway, in a bunker, or from the rough.

On some golf courses there is heather to contend with, making a recovery shot even more difficult. Nevertheless, the same method as when playing out of long grass should be employed, with the club being taken up rather than back. But let me stress again that the methods used for getting the ball out of long grass or from heather should never, I repeat never, be employed on the fairways except for playing pitch shots and even then the club should not be taken back nearly as steeply.

A common fault in recovery shots is to have the face of the club too open under the mistaken impression that the more loft one can get the better. In point of fact, what usually happens when the face is open is that the grass wraps itself round the neck of the club and so causes it to open even more. The result is a bad shot.

There will be times when the ball is found to be teed up in the rough. Then you must be bold and play an ordinary shot, just as if you were playing from the fairway. Eye and timing must be first-class, and you must never hurry the shot. Many people will try to snatch at the ball when it is lying up, with the inevitable result that the clubhead goes underneath the ball, lifting it only a little way in the air to plop down close by and almost certainly in an even worse spot.

Trees are another notorious hazard likely to be encountered on many courses and here, if your ball is some distance behind a tree, you have to decide whether to play underneath the branches, over the top or through the leaves. For beginners, the first course of action, going underneath the branches, may be the best, even though it means going a little off line. A No 4 or a No 5 iron would seem a suitable club, depending on how the ball is lying and how far you are from the green. It should be played in the normal manner, but make sure that your hands are in front of the ball at address and that the face is slightly closed, that is, the toe of the blade just a little in front of the heel. This will help to keep the ball low. Swing in a wide arc, taking the clubhead back low (unless you are in very long grass, when that is impossible) and sweep the ball away. If the ball is lying well, the No 4 iron would probably be the better of the two, even if you have to hit the shot rather more gently than you would a normal No 4 iron shot. The one thing you must keep in mind is that the ball has to be kept low.

Playing over the top of a tall tree is enough to make most golfers nervous, let alone those who have just taken up the game, and one should be very confident of one's ability before attempting such a difficult shot. Obviously, the deepest-faced iron in your bag is the club to use and it should be played as if the ball were lying in long grass. If the shot is successful, it is something to be proud of, but beginners would be well advised to regard it as a desperate sort of shot only to be attempted in a 'do or die' effort to reach the green.

Very much the same applies to a shot played through the leaves of a tree, but there may be occasions when you are not quite behind the tree and the leaves in your line are not very thick. Club selection depends on how far you are from the green, but as a rule it is best to use one without a great deal of loft because, in such circumstances, it is amazing how high the ball goes. And remember that the shot must be powerful enough to force the ball through the obstacles in its path.

In golf, it seldom pays to be foolhardy and rather than risk desperate shots one should always consider the alternative way of getting out of trouble by playing out sideways to get on the fairway or, if you are on the fairway but still behind a tree, into the middle of the fairway. You may not get much in the way of distance but at least you will have set yourself up for the next shot. And this setting yourself up for the next shot is something that should be constantly in your mind when playing a round of golf, whether or not you are in trouble. 'Planning a round', the experts call it.

15. GETTING OUT OF BUNKERS

Bunkers are the most common hazard to be found on a golf course. True, there are some courses with no bunkers at all. Berkhamsted, in Hertfordshire, is perhaps the best known of British courses in this respect, but most courses do have bunkers, many bunkers, and I have even heard of one course that has 365 of them, one for every day of the year! Fortunately, most courses have far fewer than that but, even so, almost every golfer will tell you that there are far too many bunkers around. That may be so but there they are and we must come to terms with bunkers, or sand traps as Americans call them.

One of the great differences between good golfers and the more modest members of the fraternity is in bunker play. Good players are very good at getting out of sand, poor players are not. And one of the reasons for the difference is that on the one hand there is confidence and on the other there is not. Another reason is that good players know exactly how to tackle the job, while poor players are inclined to trust to luck, and luck alone will not remove the ball from a bunker—unless it runs into one and miraculously runs out again!

When the beginner or a poor golfer goes up and sees his ball in the bunker his one idea may be to get the shot over and done with as quickly as possible, and that is a bad way to tackle a shot that requires great care and concentration. Worse still, when they see the ball lying there they may think that it can best be extricated by striking it a hard and swift blow with the deepest-faced club in the bag. But that is not at all what should be done, except perhaps if the sand in the bunker is very hard and you are lying a long way from the green. Then, perhaps, the ball can be clipped out.

Better, however, to forget this clipping-out business and get down to real bunker shots with the right kind of club, a blaster which has a very deep face. If you do not possess a blaster or something similar, go out and buy one. The purchase will repay you handsomely, for remember that every year you play golf you are going to go into perhaps hundreds of bunkers and if you do not have the right tool you are not going to be able to do the extrication job properly.

Let us assume then that clip shots are out and your club is a blaster, or the deepest-faced club you possess, When you take it in your hand you must feel confident. Don't think, if the bunker is at the side of the green, that the ball will go flying over the back of it. That will only induce timidity with the shot and the ball will probably still be in the bunker after you have hit it. Yet on the other hand, if the bunker is a long way from the green, you must not try to clip it out, especially if the sand is soft. Plenty of confidence, then, but no gambling on a hundred to one chance.

The grip should be the one you use normally, but in playing bunker shots make sure that the grip of the left hand is firmer than for normal shots. It is the only time, perhaps, that the left should really dominate the right to quite an extent—except for that personal cure for fluffed chip shots previously mentioned. The hands should normally be almost at the end of the shaft, but for little shots from shallow bunkers the hands can be some way down the shaft.

The stance should be an open one, with the left foot drawn back from the intended line of flight. Or, in other words, drawn back from a line between where the ball is lying and where you want to send it. The ball should be at a central point between the two feet, which should be firmly anchored in the sand.

Most professionals when writing instruction articles almost

always say the same thing, that in a bunker shot the club should be taken back steeply and then brought down about two inches behind the ball. No doubt this works for good golfers, but I am not so sure that it does for those who are unable to judge just what two inches mean in terms of bringing down a golf club in what, after all, is just a split second.

The experts, of course, will say: 'Well perhaps you can't bring the head of the golf club down exactly two inches behind the ball, but you can keep your eye on a certain spot in the sand and aim for that.' Well, to most of us one grain of sand looks very much like another, and the best we can do is to try to bring the head of the club down to hit the sand approximately two inches behind the ball. It has to be remembered that, with an upright swing, most golfers are concentrating on bringing down the clubhead at maximum speed, so that the spot 'two inches behind the ball' could easily be one or even four inches. To me, it all seems rather a hit or miss business and partly responsible for so many golfers being still in the sand after their first effort to get out.

Moreover, if you watch many famous golfers playing recovery shots from bunkers you will see that they do not hit the ball with one enormous thump at all. They stand well away from the ball, not over it, and they do not dig down into the sand behind the ball. In fact, they skim the club through the sand more often than not. There may be times when they dig down behind the ball, but to do that successfully calls for great accuracy, which is why digging down is not to be recommended for less accomplished golfers. If the ball is half buried, then, of course, it has to be dug out, but if it is lying on top of the sand and the sand is dry, you should try the skimming shot which some professionals refer to as 'the frying-pan shot'. In this the ball is swished away, with the deep-faced club skimming the sand just underneath the surface. There is no need to take a steep swing— in fact, if you do, you will certainly not play the shot success-fully.

Let us look again at the ingredients for this type of bunker shot. An open stance, very open. Standing well away from the ball. A grip in which the left hand is dominant. The face of the club laid open; this means that the point of the clubface is further back than the heel and it is this position of the clubface which has given the shot its 'frying pan' name. And remember that the clubhead must move fast enough to go through the sand and slide under the ball with such force that it will rise in the way you want it to.

But the shot does not end there. The club must be carried right on to a position where the face of the club is pointing towards the face of the player. If it is pointing any other way the shot has not been played successfully. Incidentally, the backswing should be quite long, otherwise you will not get sufficient power into your movement of the club.

No doubt many golfers, especially those with some experience at the game, will hesitate to attempt such a shot because they feel they should do what they have probably read or been told to do: take the club up steeply and bring it down with an enormous blow, striking the sand two inches behind the ball. If the sand is wet and heavy this method will work, but if it is dry the 'frying pan' shot is the thing. It may take some time to acquire the knack but given plenty of practice it will bring results. The blade of the club must, of course, make contact with the sand some distance behind the ball, the distance depending on the quality and state of the sand and on the power with which you drag down the clubhead.

To become a good golfer you must be able to (i) get out of a bunker the first time (or almost always the first time, because sometimes the ball is lying so badly that it is almost impossible to move it), and (ii) attain such a degree of accuracy in playing bunker shots that if you happen to be in a greenside bunker you not only get the ball on the green but near the flag. The same accuracy must be attained if there are more bunkers or other hazards beyond the one from which you are playing, for it does morale no good at all if the ball simply goes from one bunker to another.

Perhaps you have been told, or have read somewhere, that to get out of a bunker you have to take a lot of sand. I can only say that if you are bent on doing that the chances are you will take far too much and the club will have insufficient strength left to hit the ball. So don't think about taking sand, but try to concentrate on skimming the club along the sand just below the surface. And don't try to give the sand a great thump, just move the clubhead fast, and you will find that the ball will stop quite quickly—which is all-important if the bunker you are in is close to the green.

Finally, I would strongly advise you to spend as much time as you can spare in practising bunker shots—if this is at all possible. I say 'if this is at all possible' because, through sheer shortsightedness, far too many clubs do not have a practice bunker. The only alternative—and I must admit that it is frowned upon by golf club officials—is to wait until there is nobody on the course and then sneak out to some quiet bunker and practise getting out of it. But do remember to smooth out the sand after every shot, otherwise the next person who goes into that bunker during a round might well land in your foot-marks. In fact, you should smooth out your footmarks after every bunker shot during a round, and smooth them out carefully, too, not just give the sand a casual scrape.

16. UPHILL–DOWNHILL

If golf courses were flat, with no undulations, they would be very uninteresting and hardly worth playing on. The early pioneers of the game realised this and when they sought out land on which to indulge in their new-found game they chose ground which would give them variety and provide them with a challenge. The skill with which they did this has been handed down as a legacy to succeeding generations, so that either all golf courses have natural undulations or some hard-hearted golf-course architect soon sees to it that artificial mounds and hollows are made to add variety to the course—not to mention the problems of those who play on it.

Uneven lies, when the ball is resting on some kind of slope, present special problems, not only because of the lie of the ball but also because of the awkward stance which has to be adopted. For instance, when playing shots from slopes the feet are either above the ball, below it, or one foot is higher than the other. Obviously, therefore, something has to be done to deal with these different situations.

Let us start with the one where the ball is lying on an up slope, that is when the slope runs from left down to right as you play the shot. This is the easiest of all the shots which have to be played from uneven lies, mainly because there is no difficulty in taking back the clubhead. A snag, however, is that because the left foot is higher than the right, there is a great tendency to pull the ball round to the left. This is because, the weight being on the right foot, many beginners tend to have a flat swing—the club is swung round the shoulders rather than being taken back and up as for ordinary shots. If the ordinary swing which I described earlier is carried out, the ball should then go off in the desired direction. Some say that the way to counteract this drawing or pulling the ball to the left is to have an open stance (the left foot pulled further back to the intended flight than is the right), the idea being that the arc of the swing will then be restricted and the clubhead will come down more steeply than it would in the ordinary way.

But that seems to me to be introducing a fault to cure a fault and a far simpler way of sending the ball away in the right direction would be to aim a little to the right of the target. There should be no real need to do this, but if you are one of those who do find that the ball flies off to the left, try facing round a bit. But before you try experiments, check your grip to make sure that both hands are well on top of the shaft. If they are and you take back the club low along the ground and then up, you should get good results. And see, too, that your balance is correct and has not been upset by the weight going back on the lower (right) foot.

A much more difficult shot is that which has to be played when the ball is lying on a down slope. Here you have to pick up the ball smartly, so the first thing to do is to choose a club with some loft. This is not an easy shot for wooden clubs, and one should be very wary of using them in this situation. It is also one occasion (another is when your ball is lying in long grass) when the clubhead cannot be taken back as low as usual, for the simple reason that the slope which goes upwards from behind the ball just will not allow it. So you have to introduce a certain amount of improvisation.

With what is called a downhill lie, the left foot is the lower when you take up your stance, consequently the greater part of your body weight must be taken on the left foot. This means that you will have some trouble getting the ball into the air because, unconsciously, you will tend to hood or close the face of the club and the ball will then scurry away along the ground.

This, then, is the time for an open stance to restrict your

backswing and so enable you to bring down the head of the club from a steeper angle right into the ball. With the ground sloping upwards behind the ball there is no other option open to you. Perfect timing is necessary and if you are a shade more deliberate than usual that is not a bad thing. The great thing to remember with this shot is that because of necessity you must hit down at the ball, it does not mean that you have to dip your left shoulder and bend your left knee.

In other words do not accentuate this down business, for if you have chosen a club with sufficient loft—anything up to a No 8 iron depending on the grade of the slope—then the loft of the club will get the ball into the air. Though this shot is, admittedly, a particularly difficult one for beginners, there is no need to be nervous or afraid of it. You are going to have to play a great many of them, so you might as well get to terms with the shot as soon as possible. The right choice of club is particularly important, and it should be a deliberate shot, with the hands, or rather the fingers, in full control of the club. I mention the hands and fingers again here because, when playing a downhill shot, many think that to get the clubhead into the ball they have to lunge downwards with the right hand— probably under the shaft—doing all the work. This is not so. In golf the swing may change a little on special occasions but the grip remains constant. And in this context always remember that having one or both hands under the shaft will surely lead to trouble.

Having dealt with shots played from ground which is sloping up towards the hole or down from it, let us now consider two other problems, which an old Scots caddie once described as 'the same but different'. That is when the ball is below or above the level of your feet.

Standing above the ball, the obvious danger is that you may not get right down to it but may strike the ball on the top, or near the top. It will help to avoid this danger if the knees are well flexed, and you put more weight on the heels than you would normally. As you are standing above the ball it is difficult to get the clubhead straight back, and that means that a slice or the possibility of a slice is never far away. It is a good thing, therefore, to aim to the left of the target, although if you have got to that stage of efficiency when you can take the club straight back and up automatically you should not need to change direction. But to start with, anyway, it may be helpful to face just a little bit to the left.

One rule common to all shots played from uneven lies is that the head must be kept right down, and that after the ball is struck the clubhead must be taken right through. In other words, don't try to punch the ball with the clubhead stopping after it has made contact with the ball.

Now to the last of the four situations, where the ball is lying on a slope and is higher than the feet. Apart from the shot where the ground slopes up from the target, this is perhaps the most troublesome, and one where the ball so often flies off sharply to the left. This is probably because it is difficult to keep one's balance when standing below the ball, so that as you hit the ball you are liable to fall back on the right foot, or perhaps even stagger backwards. You will find that it will help you to keep your balance if you bring the feet a little closer together than usual and take a somewhat shorter grip of the club by putting the hands further down the shaft. And there is one other thing. Aim to the right of the target, because the slope of the ground being what it is, it is again difficult to get your mind into a state to tell you that you can take the clubhead straight back—the very way you are standing is all against this—so make sure you face slightly more to the right than usual and so aim to the right of the target.

This is the kind of shot in which you can employ any club you wish, providing the ball is lying well, and there can be a great deal of satisfaction in using a No 3 wood to sweep the ball away when it is lying above the level of your feet. Providing you take a slightly shorter grip, keep your feet just a little closer than normal and face to the right, you should be able to get good results.

The kind of lies discussed in this chapter may not be met with in every round, but when they are encountered do not imagine that your whole swing has to be changed. You may well have to make some adjustments to the swing, as when the ground is sloping up behind the ball, but these should not be major changes. Remember that the game of golf from tee to green is based on one method of hitting the ball, and that if you desert that principle and make changes for every shot you cannot hope to achieve any success at it. If only more golfers remembered that they would get far better results.

17. PLAYING IN WIND

A great many golfers, faced with the problem of playing into a strong wind, consider it to be a new situation and say 'Ah, now I must alter my swing to get that ball off its mark.'

How wrong they are, The swing is the same as if there were no wind at all. But what you do change is the position of the ball in relation to the feet. It should be a little further back, and if you are on the tee commonsense will tell you that the ball should be teed lower than usual. Also a stance a little wider than usual may help you to feel that your feet are more firmly anchored to the ground. This may only be psychological, but it works.

An important point to remember when you are playing into wind on the fairway is that the face of the club should not be open, or laid back. Indeed, if anything, it should be hooded or closed, by which is meant that the toe of the clubhead—the end furthest away from you—is slightly more forward than the heel. You will find that making these slight changes will help you overcome a wind which is blowing in your face.

A following wind can also cause problems, and perhaps one of the biggest is that of judging distance. When playing against the wind, you play a bigger club than you would have normally played in that situation—a No 3 iron where you would normally have used a No 4 iron, or, if the wind was very strong, a No 4 wood. Conversely, with the wind in your favour, you use a smaller club than you would normally do.

The stance when playing with the wind is just the same as for an ordinary shot. Some might think it necessary to have the ball a little further forward towards the left foot. (The opposite of playing against the wind, when you can have the ball a little further back) but there would then be more risk of hitting the ball on the top and it would be best, for the beginner at all events, to maintain a normal stance until he is ready to experiment.

Playing with the wind is mostly a matter of judgement, particularly in the selection of the right club. The shots which will cause you most trouble are the short ones to the green, especially if the course is dry and the ball is inclined to run on. This can sometimes be overcome by means of a little cunning—running the ball along the ground with a No 4 or a No 5 iron. The shot calls for nice judgement in deciding just how hard the ball has to be hit, but the result is often preferable to seeing the ball land on the green, only to run right over it and disappear into the long grass behind. So never be afraid to play a shot like this if you think it is going to pay dividends.

At times the wind will be neither in your favour nor against you, but blowing either from left to right or right to left. Experts know how to deal with these situations. They fade the ball when the wind is from right to left and draw the ball when it is blowing left to right. In other words, they change their stance and their swing in order to fade or draw the ball intentionally.

To explain how this is done would only be confusing to beginners who are likely to find that plenty of their shots are going to the left or to the right without any conscious effort on their part. Instead, I would recommend that, until more expertise is gained, these side-wind shots should be played normally, except that when the wind is blowing from left to right you aim for the left side of the fairway, and when it is blowing from right to left you aim for the right side of the fairway.

Wind and rain are often companions, and when rain has made the ground soft and heavy, it is more difficult to get the ball up into the air. The answer is to play a more lofted club than you would normally use, even though it means you will lose some distance. A bad shot will then only result in the ball going along the ground, and with the grass wet and the ground heavy it will not run very far. When playing in rain your clothing should be such as will keep you dry throughout the round, and you should always carry a small towel with which to dry the grips of the clubs before you play shots. Many beginners at golf are apt to regard this as an affectation beloved of good golfers, but I can assure them that it is not so.

18. GETTING THE BEST OUT OF PRACTICE

Many golfers never go out and practice. They are mostly those who think that practice is one long bore, and as they have no great ambitions in the game they content themselves with playing rounds of golf and leaving it at that. That is their affair, but for those who want to improve at the game practice is a necessity, and can be of immense value providing the person who is practising knows what he or she is doing.

The two main reasons why one should go out on the practice ground is to perfect shots which are almost but not quite right, and to try to correct some bad fault or faults which have crept into one's game. A third reason is in order to keep one's game at a high pitch, and it is this perhaps which attracts more good players than modest players to the practice ground.

Before going out on the practice ground anyone beginning the game should have a clear idea of what he is trying to achieve, and one of the times when practice is most valuable is after having had a lesson from the professional. The expert has been teaching one facet of the game, perhaps, the grip, or the stance, or the swing, and while everything he has said is fresh in the mind is the best time to put what he has been saying into practice. In fact, I would say that for those who can afford the time, to have a lesson and then practice what the professional has been preaching not once but half-a-dozen or more times before moving on to the next lesson would be the best possible way of building their game on a really solid foundation.

For practice to be enjoyed it must be organised and it must have variety. Far too many people go out with a couple of wood clubs, which seem to be the most popular clubs to use on the practice ground, and bang away for an hour or so without a break under the mistaken impression that good wood club shots are the key to good golf. The organisation side includes building up a supply of old golf balls, unless you are fortunate enough to belong to a club where the professional hires out golf balls at so much a hundred. In some such clubs you can even leave them where you have hit them and are spared the chore I have always found hard to bear of going round picking them up.

When you go to the practice ground at the golf club remember it is not only for your use. If there are others on it, stand well away from your neighbours. You will not then be tempted to look at what they are doing and neither will you be nearly so embarrassed as if they were standing a few feet from you.

For those beginning golf, I would advise starting practising with the more lofted irons, unless, of course, you have just been having lessons with the woods. I recommend this because the lofted face of irons such as the No 5, the No 6 or the No 7 inspires confidence in the beginner and also because, with the short irons, it is possible to aim at a target. The target may be an imaginary one but it is better to place a couple of clubs lying across each other, or stick a little piece of wood, a bit of a branch, perhaps, into the ground, and make that the object to aim at. Aiming at a target is far better than just banging away aimlessly into space, which is the kind of thing that can make practice so boring.

When indulging in this 'target' practice it will be helpful if you measure the distance between yourself and the target. When you start off with, say, a No 7 iron, stand sufficiently far from the target so that if you hit a good shot you will land in its vicinity. To start with, you may find you are too near or too far from the target and by a process of trial and error, and by pacing the distance to where the ball lands, you will eventually discover just how many yards you can hit a good shot with consistency. Having established the distance you can hit a good No 7 iron, then, gradually, you can stand a little further back and build up the length of your shots. Eventually you can do the same with every club, certainly every iron club.

Of course, not all the shots you hit on the practice ground will be good ones and when a bad shot is played that is the time to pause and check up on all the factors which go to make up the golf swing. See if both hands are on top of the club, for a start. Then check your stance. Now try the swing again, remembering to take the club back as near to the ground as possible. When you have taken it back until the wrists break naturally and the club goes up, pull the club towards you and bring it down right into the back of the ball.

The main reasons for bad shots, as far as beginners are concerned, are: (i) being in such a hurry that the head is lifted and the eyes taken off the ball; (ii) that the hands have gone too far under the shaft; (iii) that the stance has been altered so that you are standing too near the ball or too far from it; and (iv) that the swing has been too hurried. These are the principal reasons for a bad shot, while others include swaying away from the ball, particularly swaying to the right so that if and when the clubhead does make contact with the ball all the weight is on the right side.

It may be that even when you have checked up on all the points mentioned you are still playing bad shots. If so, you should either go to a professional, which again I strongly advise you to do if you get into a tangle, or try to find the cure for yourself by trial and error and by watching other and better players.

The most common of all golf faults is probably slicing, ie, when the ball goes veering off to the right. Slicing can be caused by the stance being too open, that is, a stance in which the left foot is drawn back from the line of flight. Another cause of slicing is a bad grip, in which the left hand is too far under the shaft so that the face of the club is facing to the right as it hits the ball. But, in my opinion, the principal cause of slicing is a failure to do what I have been constantly advocating, pulling the club in towards you at the top of the backswing. The result of not doing this is that the clubhead is too far away from the body as it starts to come down and so, in an effort to get the face of the club in the right position, it is drawn across the ball from outside to in. And this action is accentuated when the stance is open. So, no open stance, the club taken back low then up, and then pulled towards the body. And watch those hands. On top of the shaft, please!

Hooking is another of the primary golf faults. Again there can be several reasons, but the main one is that the right hand is too far under the shaft. When the ball is hooked, the right hand being under the shaft causes the clubface to be hooded, which means facing the left or behind you if you like, so naturally the ball goes to the left. It is as simple as that. Also, when the right hand is under the shaft there is a tendency not to take the clubhead back and then up but back around and then around the shoulders. This means that, to make contact with the ball, a sort of a heave has to take place, and a heave with the face of the club (the part of the club you are supposed to hit the ball with) pointing to the left turns what might have been an ordinary hook into something of a real disaster.

Many novices at golf find that one of their most common faults is hitting the ball on the top, with the result that it never gets off the ground. The reason for this topping of the ball is that it is being hit on the upward swing of the clubhead and so merely trundles along the ground whereas it should have been hit when the club was at the very lowest point of the swing. A contributory cause is swaying to the right away from the ball. So make certain that when you take the club back, the weight is on the right foot and that when the club is coming down the weight is on the left foot. But remember, too, that although when taking back the club the left shoulder should be pointing to the ground, the left shoulder lifts as the club is brought down.

The opposite fault to topping is skying the ball. And that

means exactly what it says—putting the ball too high into the air. Although the results of topping and skying are very different, the wrong transference of weight is a common factor in both cases. The only difference is that, in skying the ball, the club has hit the ball fractionally early.

Another cause of skying the ball, and I believe the major one, is loss of control over the club through allowing the left arm, or possibly both arms, to become bent. This fault has already been mentioned, so make sure that in drawing the club down, you do it in one firm action with the arms and hands in full control.

If you persevere with regular practice and remember never to hurry a shot and always to keep your head down, you should be able to get your golf into shape by yourself. But if you can spare the time and the money, do try to have some lessons, not only when starting the game but also when you develop a fault which you just cannot sort out for yourself.

And one last word about practice. If you find it a bore there is really not much point in doing it all. Better to try and pick up experience as you go round a golf course and many beginners have improved their golf by doing just that.

19. HOW TO REDUCE YOUR HANDICAP

Just how much improvement can be made at golf depends entirely on the individual. Some beginners will take up the game and within a very short space of time, say about a year, they will have made substantial progress and have seen their handicap come down substantially. Others will slog on for much longer than a year and see only minimal improvement.

There are many reasons for the difference between the progress of various players. Obviously, some beginners will have more natural aptitude for the game than others. Then there is the amount of time which can be devoted to the game for even a 'natural' will have difficulty in improving if he or she is only able to fit in one game a week.

If you are fortunate enough to live near a golf course, you will perhaps be able to get in some practice in the summer evenings after you return from work. If that is impossible, then you have to make the best of things on Saturday and Sunday and, if you are really keen, to spend your holidays playing golf. The point I am trying to make is that if you want to reduce your handicap you must devote as much time as possible to playing—there is no other way.

Let us first take the case of those who can visit golf clubs more than twice a week. Assuming they have had sound grounding in the game, it is a good idea to spend many hours on the practice ground before even venturing out on the course. This may not be an easy thing to do because there will be a strong urge to get out on the course, but the more experience you have had in hitting shots before attempting to play some holes the easier and more enjoyable the round will be.

After you have been on the practice ground long enough to have acquired some degree of confidence, you can then try a few holes by yourself and later go out with a friend, or perhaps some kindhearted fellow member who has the patience to encourage you and give you a few simple hints. Later on you will find that taking all kinds of advice from better players is not always the best thing to do, but at the start of your golfing career it is unlikely that you will come to any great harm by watching what your partner does and acting on any hint he or she may give you. As in learning to drive a car, a member of the family is not always the best person to teach one to play golf. They are often apt to become impatient, which may shake your confidence, so that it is generally better to rely on someone other than a close relative, if you can.

After you have been out on the course a few times with some tolerant person, the next stage will be to move on, as it were, and to start playing with various people. You will find that there are usually golfers willing to help you, and you should always try to play with better players than yourself. You will by now know quite a bit about the game and be able to hit at least a fair number of satisfactory shots, and it is then that you will really start enjoying yourself. And, strange as it may sound, it will not be long before you see other people out on the course who are worse than you are—which will help to sustain you greatly.

If you are young, it may be that the club you have joined has a junior section—in which case you are in clover. Most junior sections offer reduced subscription rates and all run their own special competitions in which, as you progress, you will be able to play, as well as in open junior competitions.

When you become fairly proficient and have been given a club handicap, you should play in as many club competitions as you can. By doing so, you will be recording every score, and will be able to monitor your progress. Perhaps the biggest thrill will come on the day when you return a card of less than a hundred. There are few moments in golf quite like that one.

In handicaps, the usual limit for men is 24—sometimes 18. For women, the limit is 36. This means that if you are a man and hand in a card of 94, your nett handicap would be 70, which would be very good indeed. Everybody thus has a fair chance when playing in handicap competitions.

But do not wait for competitions to begin keeping a score for your rounds. And don't just make a mental note of it—get it down in black and white and no nonsense. Over a period, despite occasional fluctuations, you will find that the overall pattern will be an encouraging reduction in scores. Most Americans do this and look at the high standard of their golf!

Though putting is the most important part of golf, in friendly games many putts are not holed out on the greens—indeed some people do not even trouble to finish a hole. There may be occasions when someone has run into trouble and to hole out would unduly delay following players but as a general rule you should try to keep a correct score for every round. You will then be able to see just how much improvement you are making and knowledge such as this will greatly help you to reduce your handicap.

And even if you are being pressed closely by following players because you have lost ground, you can always invite them to proceed with their game, and complete the hole when they are out of range. Such a gesture will be much appreciated and you are then free to continue your game without any feeling of harassment.

Other factors which go to a reduction of handicap are the basic ones: concentrating on each shot, knowing exactly what you are trying to do, not hurrying, forgetting the occasional bad shot, and remembering that, in golf, the great thing is 'keeping the ball in play'. Which means not visiting bunkers or putting the ball into clumps of trees or suchlike hazards.

This is not, however, to suggest that beginners should be timid in their play. Hitting the ball a little way along the fairway is all very fine, and if backed up by good putting can be the foundation of steady scores, but it is not the way to become a good player because the shots to the green and the putting cannot be relied upon to be perfect all the time and lack of distance will eventually take its toll of your game, and your handicap. Be cautious at first by all means but do not make the mistake of all too many beginners of setting your sights too low and being content with a lower standard of golf than you know you are capable of achieving.

All of which adds up to the conclusion that the extent to which you can reduce your handicap and the speed with which you can do it, depends almost entirely on what you want out of golf and how much time you can, or are prepared to spend in playing it.

20. ENJOY YOUR GOLF

Despite all the misfortune which can and does happen to golfers in the course of a round, it is only occasionally and when a game has gone exceptionally badly that anybody will come back into the clubhouse saying that he has hated every minute of the round.

True, there are bad moments but golfers, being great optimists, prefer to remember the good ones—and as they expand on them in the club bar to anybody who will listen, it will appear that even the bad moments were due to blows from fate rather than to rank bad shots. They find enjoyment, too, in replaying their round in retrospect and, not least, from having seen other golfers on the course who were playing much worse than they were. For, in the main, golfers are selfish people whose chief preoccupation is with their own game.

But out on the course the best way to enjoy your golf is to be completely relaxed. If you take your personal or business worries out on the course with you then the chances are that you will play bad golf. It may not be easy to forget the cares of the world and thrust them to the back of your mind when you are out on the course, but if you can you will play better golf and certainly enjoy your round a great deal more.

It may be that some who read this are taking up golf fairly late in life and have no great ambitions. Perhaps they are turning to the game after their more active sports days are over as a congenial form of exercise. True, they want to play a reasonable game but, wisely, they will not strive for perfection for only in comparatively few cases can that be achieved by those who take up the game at an age much beyond, say, forty-five. Even so, such people, especially if they have been sports players in their younger days, can reach a very fair standard of play and there are many cases of former footballers and the like starting golf rather younger than forty-five, say thirty-five, who have become very good golfers indeed.

What I am really saying is that if you take up golf in middle age with exercise as the aim, be content with a modest standard and do not try for something which is out of reach. Far too many such players start to experiment with this and that new method, always trying to find one which will enable them to perform miracles on the course. And at the end of it all they are little better than when they started.

What they would be much better advised to do is to adopt a good sound method, master it thoroughly, and then to stick to it. They have to realise that they are probably no longer as strong as they were and, that being so, they must build on what they have got. If they do that they should continue to make a modest improvement at the game, and certainly enough for them to enjoy their golf.

I have played golf almost all my life and find now that my long game is shorter than it was, so that I have to rely more and more on my short game. And that is what people who take up the game late in life should try to achieve. They will then find that they can save many strokes around and on the green and will be surprised just how well they can hold their own with younger golfers who can hit the ball much further.

And younger players, too, should by no means neglect the short game. The joy of hitting the ball a long way is immense, but the joy soon fades after a fluffed chip followed by three putts.

But whether young or middle-aged, and whether the aim is to be very good or just to play a decent game, it is essential to start off with the best equipment you can afford and then to look after it well. I always think my car runs better if it is clean, and though I know the feeling is purely psychological,

I have the same feeling when playing golf—that I play better when all my equipment is in good order.

Take shoes, for instance. These are very important in playing golf, yet one so often sees golfers going out to play in battered old shoes, and dirty shoes at that. Ideally, they should be watertight and the studs which give a grip on the ground should be all in place and not worn. Above all, shoes must be comfortable. Golf clothing should be able to keep out cold and should not be too tight—you cannot swing a golf club properly in tight clothing.

Rain is a particular bugbear to golfers, so good waterproof clothing is essential, and when you finish a round which has been played in the rain see that you dry your clothing and clean your shoes after they have been dried. Nowadays a wide selection of golf clothing is available from sports shops and in the shops of club professionals, and it would be a false economy not to buy the best you can afford.

The aim of every beginner will be to join a golf club, and this may call for patience in areas where all the clubs have a full membership. You may at least, however, be able to get your name on the waiting-list, and until you are able to join, you will probably be able to find a public course on which you can play on payment of a fee. Games on such a course can be varied with visits to private clubs, most of which allow visitors to play on payment of what is known as a green fee. This varies from club to club but as a rule is not too high during the week. At weekends many clubs discourage visitors by charging a very high fee for Saturday and Sunday play.

Many golfers, whether or not they are members of clubs, belong to golfing societies which arrange golf outings from time to time. Such societies might be for employees of firms, for School Old Boys' Associations or, indeed, might have been formed by a band of mutual acquaintances. Perhaps your office has such a society or your old school. These society meetings can be great fun, as well as enabling you to meet fellow workers socially or to renew acquaintances with old school friends or with fellow members of some organisation or association to which you belong.

And when you do eventually become a member of a golf club, make sure that you join in the social activities of the club and meet other members. Too often the same members tend always to play golf with each other. This is bad for their golf, because they get to know each other's game too well, and it is also anti-social. Many golfers, especially the older ones, may not agree with this, feeling no doubt that they have already made all the friends they want, but the fact remains that one of the things which can make golf so enjoyable is the opportunity it provides for making new friends.

And make no mistake, golf is a game to be enjoyed whether you are intent on reaching the top flight or whether your sights are set more modestly. Players in both categories have been known to become so worried by their game that they reached a stage when it was sheer agony to them. Better then, to try never to worry too much about bad shots or a bad round, and to remember what the great American, Lloyd Magrum, said to me many years ago: 'It's not your wife, it's not your life, it's only a game.'

GLOSSARY

ALBATROSS: A hole achieved in three strokes under bogey or (in United States) par.

ARC (of the swing): The groove in which the head of the golf club moves during the swing.

BETTER BALL: A competition in which two partners play as a team, the better score of either counting.

BIRDIE: The score for the hole which is one under bogey or (in United States) par.

BLASTER: A deep-faced club used for recovery shots, mostly from bunkers and sometimes from long grass.

BLIND (Hole or shot): A blind hole is one in which the green cannot be seen from the tee. A blind shot is when some high object prevents the player from seeing where he intends to hit the ball.

BOGEY: The score for each hole which would be taken by a scratch golfer in his normal form, taking into account average playing conditions. Now bogey has been superseded to some extent by the Standard Scratch Score, or par, which is calculated by other means.

BOUNDARY: The perimeter or outside limits of the golf course.

BRASSIE: The old name for a No 2 wood, so-called because the clubs had a brass sole for making shots off the fairway easier.

BUNKER: A hazard filled with sand. Bunkers are to be found at strategic points on the fairway and on the sides of the fairway. They are usually more numerous around the green for the purpose of trapping an inaccurate shot.

BYE: The number of holes remaining to be played when a match is finished. Often in friendly games there is a little wager on who can win the bye, or remaining holes.

CADDIE: A person who carries a golfer's clubs. The word 'caddie' is derived from an old French word meaning young boy or 'cadet'.

CADDIE-CART: Much used nowadays; and usually a two-wheeled container pulled by hand. Caddie carts are also known as trolleys. There are also trolleys with electric motors which can either be guided like a milk float and even (mostly in the USA) electric trolleys which can carry two golfers as well as their bags of clubs.

CASUAL WATER: After heavy rain, water frequently appears in pools on some golf courses. If the ball goes into such a pool it can be lifted without penalty. If the accumulation of water is not apparent but appears as the golfer takes up his stance, a lift and drop is still permissible.

CHIP: The name for a little lofted shot to the green. It is employed mainly in order that the ball may be played over a bunker, or other hazard.

CONCEDE: A hole is conceded when one player has played so many strokes that it is impossible to win it from his opponent. He then picks up his ball thus indicating to his opponent that he has given up the hole. A player may also concede a putt to his opponent if he feels the opponent is certain not to miss it.

COURSE: The ground over which golf is played. A golf course is usually of eighteen holes, but there are also many nine-hole courses which are played over twice to make up the eighteen holes if desired. Courses consist of tees, fairways, greens, rough and other hazards, some of which are man-made and others which are natural.

DEAD: When the ball lands so near the hole that it is all but impossible for the putt to be missed. There is no specific distance for ruling whether a ball is dead or not.

DIVOT: The piece of turf which is cut out by the club striking the ball a descending blow. Moderate golfers rarely take a divot. But if a slice of turf has been removed, it must be replaced and stamped down to avoid damage to the course.

DORMIE: A golfer is deemed to be dormie, or dormy, if he or he and his partner are as many holes up as there remain to be played in a round, eg, if one side were four holes up and four holes remained to be played they would be dormie. The opponent could not then win the round, but could, of course, win all the remaining holes and halve the match.

DRAW: To give spin on the ball when striking it so as to make it come in from right to left.

EAGLE: A score for the hole which is two better than bogey or (in the USA) par.

ECLECTIC: This is the score at each hole taken from two or more rounds of golf, eg, if a golfer scored a three at the first hole and in other rounds had a higher score, the three would be the eclectic (or chosen) score. Popular at some clubs.

FAIRWAY: The cut portion of the course between the teeing ground and the green.

FLAGSTICK: The pole, or post usually with a small flag attached placed in the hole so that it provides the target for golfers to aim at.

FLUFF (or DUFF): A bad shot during which the club hits the ground rather than the ball. The latter then falls short of the intended distance.

FORE: A shout of warning to indicate to anyone on the course that a ball is going in their direction.

FOUR-BALL: Such matches are greatly to the liking of club golfers. In a four-ball match the pairs play as teams with the lower score of the two partners counting as the score at the hole. In the United States, it is known as a Scotch Foursome.

FOURSOMES: Four players go out together, each pair playing as a team, but instead of playing their own ball they play alternate shots with the same ball and drive at alternate holes.

GREEN: The term 'green' once used to describe the entire course. Now 'green' is the word used to describe the putting surfaces on the course.

GREENSOME: A form of foursome sometimes played in which players go out in fours, two players playing as a team. All four players drive and then each team can choose which ball to play for the remainder of the hole.

GROUND UNDER REPAIR: Ground which has been repaired by greenkeepers. The area is usually marked by a notice, and it is permissible to lift and drop the ball without penalty.

HALVED: A hole is halved, or a match is halved, when the opponents are level, either in relation to the strokes taken at each hole or, in the case of a match when, at the end, the players are level.

HANDICAP: All golfers are given a handicap after they join a golf club. The handicap is based on scores returned after a few rounds. The usual limit for men is 24 (sometimes 18) and for women 36.

HANGING LIE: When the ball is lying in such a position that it is on a downward slope.

HAZARD: Any obstacle, such as a bunker or a ditch.

HEAD: That part of the club with which the ball is struck.

HOLE: The hole is the target on the green at which all golfers aim. It is required to be 4in in diameter and at least 4in deep.

HOLING-OUT: When the ball is actually put into the hole. The term 'holing-out' is sometimes used to mean that a player has holed in a certain score at a given hole.

HONOUR: The preference given to the player whose turn it is to drive first. The honour on the first tee can be agreed. At other holes the honour goes to the player who has had the lowest score at the previous hole.

IDENTIFICATION: Making certain that the ball about to be played is the one belonging to the player who is playing the shot. The golf ball must not be lifted except in instances when it is not possible to identify it in any other way.

LADIES' TEE: The teeing ground used by women golfers. It is almost always some distance in front of the men's tee. Ladies' handicaps are calculated from these tees.

LATERAL WATER HAZARD: A stream or ditch which runs along the course instead of across it. Special rules apply.

LIFT AND DROP: When for some reason the ball has to be lifted because it is not possible to play it from the position in which it lies. Usually there is a penalty for lifting and dropping, but not always.

LIKE AS WE LIE: When each player has played the same number of strokes for a hole. 'Playing the like' is to play a stroke which, after being played, brings your score for the hole to the same number of strokes played by your opponent up to that point.

LINKS: When golf was first played it was at the seaside, and golf courses there became known as links.

LOCAL RULES: Golf everywhere is played according to the rules laid down, in the United States by the United States Golf Association, but elsewhere as laid down by the Royal and Ancient Club of St Andrews. But all clubs have their own set of 'local rules' on points which, because of local conditions, apply to golf on their particular course.

LOFT: The angle at which the clubhead lies in relation to the shaft. The loft increases in degree from the straight-faced driver down to the wedge. Putters are straight faced.

LOST BALL: When a golf ball is lost golfers are allowed five minutes to look for it, but after that time they have to deem it lost and play another according to the rules.

MATCH PLAY: When opponents play against each other, the winner being the one who has won more holes than the other.

MEDAL PLAY: Medal play is a competition in which the number of strokes taken during the round, or score, counts. Monthly medal competitions are a feature of all golf clubs. Medal play is another expression meaning stroke play as distinct from match play.

NIBLICK: A name used in the old days for the deep-faced club used for short shots to the green or for getting out of hazards or long grass.

OBSTRUCTIONS: Objects, either movable or immovable, which prevent the playing of a shot.

OUT OF BOUNDS: When the ball is played outside the perimeter of the course, or hole, thus incurring a penalty.

OUTSIDE AGENCY: When a ball, having been played, is removed by a person or animal, the latter is called an outside agency.

PAR: This is the score allocated to a hole or to a course. It is sometimes identified with the Standard Scratch Score and based on the terrain of the course, the length of the holes and other factors.

PARTNER: The person with whom one plays in a stroke competition or as a team in a foursomes competition.

PENALTY: When a shot is played into a lie from which it is unplayable or out of bounds, a penalty is incurred according to the rules of the game. It can also be incurred for an infringement of the rules.

PLACING: There are certain circumstances in which a ball may be replaced, such as in a waterlogged bunker. These instances are very rare and any placing of the ball must be in strict accordance with the rules of the game.

PLAYING THE ODD: If you are level on strokes with your opponent and you play one more shot to bring your total to one more than your opponent, this is playing the odd.

PLAYING OUT OF TURN: If a player plays out of turn, either on the tee or the fairway, his opponent may require the ball to be called back and the shot replayed.

PLUS-FOURS: Wide, fully-cut knickerbockers developed from the old Norfolk knickerbockers worn by the earlier golfers. Now worn by a few golfers in Britain mostly in winter when courses are wet.

PUTT: The stroke used on the putting surface of the course, ie, the greens. The club used for the stroke is a putter.

ROUND: Playing all the holes on the course, usually 18 holes, but, in the case of 9-hole courses, half this number.

RUB OF THE GREEN: Any interference with the ball which can be put down to fate.

RULES OF THE GAME: The rules under which golf is played.

SAND WEDGE: One of the clubs used for recovery shots from bunkers.

SCORECARD: The card taken out and marked by golfers during a round. It has to be filled in by a golfer's partner, checked and signed by both players.

SINGLE: A match in which two players are opposed to each other.

SLOT: To hole a putt confidently.

SPOON: The old name for a No 3 wood. It has more loft in the face than a No 2 wood and is generally used for shots from the fairway. It is also used from the tee, particularly by golfers of moderate attainment.

SQUARE: When the clubface is facing the target at impact. At the top of the swing the club is neither pointing to the ground nor towards the sky. The word 'square' can also be used to describe a game in which players are level. A square stance is when both feet, both hips and both shoulders are aligned to the intended flight of the ball.

STABLEFORD: A system for competition invented by Dr Frank Stableford in which points are scored for the number of strokes taken at each hole. One point is scored for a hole done in one shot over bogey, two points for equalling bogey, three points for one less than bogey and so on. No points are awarded for a hole done in more than one over bogey. A player's club handicap is used in the system.

STANDARD SCRATCH SCORE: *See* 'Par'.

STROKE: The hitting of the ball during the club swing.

STROKE COMPETITION: *See* 'Medal play'.

TEE: The wooden or plastic peg on which the ball is placed prior to driving off. In the old days tees were merely little piles of sand. Tee is also used to describe the teeing ground.

TEEING GROUND: The part of the course used for driving from— a rectangular space with at least two club lengths to the rear of the two tee-markers.

TEE-MARKERS: Metal or plastic objects used to mark the forward limit of the teeing ground.

TEE-PEGS: *See* 'Tee'.

THREE-BALL: A match in which three players are involved, each playing his own ball.

THREESOME: A match in which three players are involved. One plays against the other two who play alternate shots with the one ball.

TIE: A team match (involving several golfers on each side) which finishes level.

THROUGH THE GREEN: The situation which arises when a golfer has played a shot which is too strong and the ball has gone over the green. It is also the term used in the rules to refer to the whole area of the course except the teeing ground and putting green of the hole being played and all hazards on the course.

TRAP: The American term for a bunker.

TROLLEY: *See* 'Caddie cart'.

UNPLAYABLE BALL: When the ball lies in such a position that it is impossible to hit it. It has then to be lifted and dropped in accordance with the rules.

WEDGE: The modern, deep-faced club with a broad sole for playing a high shot or pitch to the green, often with spin imparted to the ball.

WINTER RULES: Rules for play during the months when the course is wet. Winter rules entail rolling over the ball with the clubhead so as to ensure a better lie and thus lessen the damage to the turf. This can also be called a 'preferred lie'. Winter rules can also permit the cleaning of the ball.

INDEX